6/90 $17.94

The Awakening
of the Soviet Union

The Awakening
of the Soviet Union

GEOFFREY HOSKING

HARVARD UNIVERSITY PRESS
CAMBRIDGE, MASSACHUSETTS

1990

In memory of Kostya Bogatyrev
who did not live to see it

Copyright© 1990 by Geoffrey Hosking
All rights reserved
Printed in the United States of America
10 9 8 7 6 5 4 3 2 1

This book is printed on acid-free paper, and its binding
materials have been chosen for strength and durability.

Library of Congress Cataloging-in-Publication Data

Hosking, Geoffrey A.
The Awakening of the Soviet Union / Geoffrey Hosking.
p.   cm.
ISBN 0-674-05550-0 (alk. paper)
1. Soviet Union—Politics and government—1985–   2. Perestroĭka.
3. Soviet Union—Intellectual life—1970–   4. Soviet Union—Social
life and customs—1970–   I. Title.
DK288.H67   1990
947.085—dc20

89-38876
CIP

Contents

Preface

Most studies of the exciting changes taking place in the Soviet Union focus on Gorbachev and the reform programme he has launched. That is understandable, but it nevertheless gives a misleadingly one-sided view of the situation. The present book grew out of my desire to see things from the viewpoint of the society he is trying to transform. Reform in the Soviet Union can only be initiated from above, but the vital motor lies below, among the peoples and social groups whose autonomous activity Gorbachev has encouraged.

The kernel of my ideas was contained in an inaugural lecture delivered at the University of London in February 1987. My purpose then was to counter the misleading tendency, common among western social scientists, to assume that the Soviet Union was just a variety of authoritarian regime now at last evolving into something better. At the same time, I wanted to contest the opposite image, offered us by some émigrés, of a new socio-biological species, *Homo sovieticus*, said to have been irreversibly bred by debilitating Soviet conditions, and congenitally incapable of generating any independent civic or cultural life. I was convinced, from my own experience, that the Soviet Union was a totalitarian society, but that nevertheless a kind of political emancipation was possible within it, indeed was waiting to come about. I believed that, if the then embryonic policies of glasnost and perestroika developed into real democratisation, then the Soviet peoples would prove readier to make more fruitful use of it than we in the west usually gave them credit for. The events of the last two years have borne out that assertion more emphatically than I could have conceived at the time. So it seemed worth attempting to give a fuller historical explanation for the unexpected vigour with which social movements unfolded, once they got the chance. The BBC's invitation to me to deliver the Reith Lectures in the autumn of 1988 provided the perfect opportunity. I have extensively rewritten the lectures and brought them up to date, in order to produce this book.

While putting these chapters together, I have been sorely aware of the precarious posture which the contemporary historian adopts. Much of the evidence in favour of my views has been accumulating in the last few months. That is reassuring, but poses problems of perspective. Even as I round off my writing, the turbulent proceedings of the Congress of People's Deputies fill Soviet television screens and raise the possibility that we may be moving on to a qualitatively new stage in the emergence of civil society. At such close quarters it is difficult to tell. So I am painfully conscious that my judgements may prove fallible.

I am very grateful to the staff of the Library of the School of Slavonic & East European Studies who have provided for most of my needs in the way of documentation, supplemented by the library of the London School of Economics, and by the archives of Radio Liberty in Munich, and of the Forschungsstelle Osteuropa at Bremen University. My efforts to follow the tracks of so many heavenly bodies simultaneously would have been in vain without the help of numerous colleagues. The SSEES Soviet Press Study Group has furnished me with abundant information and opinion every Wednesday lunchtime. Shirin Akiner, Jane Ellis, Peter Frank and Bob Service have read earlier drafts and offered valuable advice and suggestions. Nora Beloff and Alex Shtromas took a lot of time and trouble to give me their views on the Reith Lectures. Some colleagues rallied round with invaluable cuttings and references, or by allowing me to see their own work in progress: Tamara Dragadze, Martin Dewhirst, Peter Duncan, Stephen Jones, Walter Laqueur and Peter Rowland. Murray Pollinger, my literary agent, steered me through the difficult transition between broadcasting and publication. Helen Fraser, Lisa Glass and Patricia Williams were encouraging and perceptive editors. I am most grateful to those numerous people in Moscow, Kiev and Tbilisi who took time off in the spring of 1988 to explain to me what was happening in their country: their personal insights form an essential part of what follows. But my greatest professional debt is to David Morton, who as BBC editor guided me through the Reith Lectures: with his perspicacity, sympathy and profound knowledge of the Soviet Union, he saved me from many errors, and sometimes spotted what I was thinking before I did.

My wife, Anne, and my daughters, Katya and Janet, have borne with an unpredictable and semi-absentee husband/father while this book was being prepared, and have nevertheless offered their love and support when it was needed. To them I owe most of all.

This book is dedicated to the memory of a friend who was murdered in Moscow ten years to the day before the Chernobyl' explosion. Paradoxically, since that terrible anniversary I have felt what he stood for come alive as never before in his own homeland: may it not be brutally cut short as his life was.

School of Slavonic & East European Studies
University of London

June 1989

1

A great power
in crisis

In the last year or two one of the most intriguing sections of any Soviet newspaper has been the readers' letters column. Take the following cry of indignation, published recently in *Pravda*: 'I cannot be silent! Look at what is going on around us. In Leningrad – the cradle of the revolution – well-fed, insolent thugs parade on the streets with swastika armbands . . . At an Estonian song contest a half-naked singer cavorts about with a cross round his neck, and this on television! In Armenia there are strikes – people skiving without any reason. Where is the law? Why is it silent? And why are those responsible for law enforcement inactive?'[1]

The writer signs himself 'Member of the Communist Party since 1945, Sverdlovsk' – the rough Soviet equivalent of 'Disgusted, Tunbridge Wells'. Life has been very unkind to such staunch party members recently. They have seen their own leadership sponsor changes which affront their most cherished beliefs. State ownership of the means of production is undermined with impunity, as they see it, by speculators and private marketeers. Rock music and western clothing are corrupting the youth. The party itself no longer seems to know where it's going: why, it's even permitted a self-styled opposition to come into existence. And, worst of all, the old stalwarts' hero, Stalin, is pilloried in the press as a mass murderer. As a Second World War invalid wrote from Kiev: 'Still as unfledged youths, we went into battle with the cry, "For the motherland, for Stalin! Hurrah!" Those were the last words that many of us ever spoke. And now you want us to blot that period out of our memories, to admit that we gave our lives or became cripples in a struggle for injustice?!'[2]

While his Tunbridge Wells counterpart works himself up over trivia, Disgusted Sverdlovsk has a real point. However blinkered his own approach to it, what he is witnessing is a real and fundamental crisis. He may blame Mr Gorbachev for it, but actually it is rooted in the very nature of the Soviet system, and Gorbachev has done no more than bring it to the surface in order to tackle it. Even so, the risks involved in his programme of radical reform are so serious that one is bound to ask: why attempt it at all? Why not just muddle on as Brezhnev did for eighteen years?

In a sense that is a real option, but muddling on would have consequences which might not be acceptable to the leaders of a great power. Largely as a result of the ambitious military and foreign policy of the Brezhnev period, the Soviet Union suffers from what the historian Paul Kennedy recently called 'imperial overstretch', that is, strategic commitments so diverse and military power so overgrown that they drain the resources of the economy on which they depend.[3] The danger has been intensified by the American Strategic Defence Initiative, which challenges the Soviet Union to develop a new generation of weapons involving lasers, supercomputers and sensitive long-range guidance systems. These are precisely the technological areas where it lags farthest behind. A nation which can outproduce the world in steel, cement and coal is, in effect, panting along one industrial revolution behind its major rivals, its preponderance in conventional arms liable to be nullified by the deployment of new weapons it cannot hope to match. If, then, the Soviet Union is to remain a great power even in the one sphere where it has hitherto excelled, the military one, it must create an economy which possesses the capacity to generate and assimilate independent technological innovation. This is the heart of the matter as all the Soviet leaders see it, whatever their shades of difference over perestroika, and that is why they are not prepared to just muddle on.

The economic deficiencies are merely part of a deeper crisis which permeates the whole society. It had already been diagnosed in 1970 by three distinguished Soviet scholars then in official disfavour: the nuclear physicist Andrei Sakharov, the historian Roy Medvedev and the mathematician Valentin Turchin. Writing to Brezhnev, they warned that the economy had entered a stage of 'dislocation and stagnation', the roots of which lay in the structure of society itself, in the 'anti-democratic norms of public life' established in the Stalin era and never properly disavowed. Without democratisation and the guarantee of civil liberties, they warned, any purely economic reforms would fall on stony ground. They proposed political reforms remarkably similar to those which Gorbachev is adopting today: greater openness, or glasnost, in public life; a press and information law; increasing the powers of the soviets as organs of self-administration; and restoring genuine elections, with multiple candidacies, in both party and soviets.[4]

There is plenty of evidence that Soviet society was ripe for such reform at the time when Sakharov and his colleagues proposed it, and it is even more so today. The Soviet Union is far from being the backward, largely peasant country it was even a generation or so ago, when de-Stalinisation was first begun. In 1960 half the Soviet population lived in the countryside: today the proportion is not more than a third, and only a quarter at most can be called peasants.[5] When one thinks of the weight of the peasant problem in Russian history, that is a momentous change. The Soviet Union is now a highly urbanised society – though one in which the peasant heritage is still strong: as recently as the late seventies half the townsfolk had been born in the villages.[6]

No less important: during the same period the Soviet Union has become a highly educated society. If in 1939 only just over 10 per cent of the population aged ten and over had secondary education (often incomplete), that figure had reached 36 per cent by 1959 and 70 per cent by 1986. And whereas in 1939 only just over half of those doing non-manual labour had any secondary education, by 1959 that proportion was 90 per cent and today is virtually 100 per cent. Over the last thirty years there has been a fourfold growth in the proportion of people with higher education, from just over two per cent in 1959 to nearly nine per cent now. An important aspect of this educational revolution is that women have partaken of it as much as men: in 1986, among the working population, the proportion of women with secondary education was virtually identical with that of men, at 88 per cent.[7] Occupationally speaking, the fastest-growing sectors of the population have been the administrative and professional strata which absorb those college graduates. They have expanded sevenfold since 1940, and the growth shows no signs of easing.[8]

This educational development is of great importance, for education in the Soviet Union is a more crucial social mechanism than it is in the west. In a society where birth and property play a minor role, educational attainment is the principal agency for the transmission from one generation to another of privilege, status and power. Admittedly, nowadays it functions in a paradoxical fashion. Whereas at one time, higher or even secondary education was sufficiently rare to guarantee high social status of itself, this has long ceased to be the case. Higher education is a necessary prerequisite for the social climber, but it is no longer sufficient. It is also much harder to achieve: the chances of getting into university are today only half what they were twenty years ago.[9] So young people have much more difficulty in attaining something which simultaneously offers fewer rewards. There has been a growth of what, in purely functional terms, one can call 'over-education', the PhD on the building site. This mismatch has engendered considerable frustration; on the other hand, it has also brought the ferment of education into relatively humble forms of employment. We may expect nowadays to see receptivity to ideas at *all* levels of urban society in the USSR.

Overall, then, even since the last round of serious reforms was attempted under Khrushchev, the Soviet social structure has become markedly more urban and professional. Now, on the face of it, a population which in education, lifestyle and occupation has become so much more like the west should be ready for an open, democratic style of politics. And indeed, there has been evidence for more than two decades that society and politics were out of phase with one another, that society was starting to outgrow the crude and rigid integument of the party-controlled political system. An unofficial or 'black' economy has been mushrooming to meet the needs which the cumbersome planned state economy left unsatisfied. Similarly, extruded by the narrow confines of the Communist political monopoly, a new kind of semi-underground politics was taking shape, which we in the west referred to as 'dissent'. And the dreary output of official culture was increasingly being challenged by the primitive technology but lively appeal of *samizdat* – self-publishing.

In this sense, we might hypothesise that Gorbachev is doing no more than belatedly bringing the political system up to date with a more developed society. Or, as one American observer has put it, that he is not so much impelling change as 'uncorking' it. [10]

But it is not as simple as that. There is no straightforward transition from social to political change. A sophisticated society is a necessary condition for sophisticated politics, but it is by no means a sufficient one.

So what stands in the way? The obstacle, as I see it, is the political system handed down from Stalin, which has proved remarkably tenacious and resistant to change. All this would be obvious enough, were it not that Sovietologists have displayed so much uncertainty about how to describe that system. Thirty years ago nearly all observers of the Soviet scene would have agreed in calling it 'totalitarian': they'd have pointed to the monopoly mass party, with its grip on all political and social institutions; the single dominant leader; the single permissible ideology; the totally controlled culture and mass media; the completely planned, centrally directed economy; and the ubiquitous and terroristic security police. [11]

Ever since Khrushchev eased the terror in the late fifties, though, there have been warnings that we were misunderstanding the country, that the term 'totalitarian' was a misnomer, a relic of Stalinism and the cold war, an obstacle to understanding a society which was becoming more open, diverse and internally differentiated. What designation might be more appropriate was widely, though inconclusively, debated: 'modernising', some thought, or 'corporatist' or 'state socialist' – even 'pluralist'.[12] There is some sense in all of these epithets, except the last, 'pluralist', which is precisely what the Soviet Union is not. But none of them has ever replaced the term 'totalitarian' as an instrument for enabling us to see the Soviet system as a whole. None of them defines the essence of the system as opposed to characterising certain of its aspects. The danger of partial labels is that they can mislead us into seeing in Soviet society superficial analogies with western institutions, precisely because we lose sight of the overall context. Terms like 'socialisation', 'public opinion' and 'interest groups' tend to degenerate into being used as if they meant roughly the same as in the United States or West Germany.

It is true that the 'totalitarian' concept has weaknesses, at any rate in the form in which it has been employed up to now. It first took hold among a generation of American scholars emerging after the Second World War, somewhat guilty about past isolationism, ready to transfer morally absolutist feelings about Nazi Germany to the new enemy, as the Soviet Union then appeared to be, and sensitive to the experience of Central European refugees who had suffered terribly at the hands of both regimes.[13] As a result the concept has tended to imply an implacably hostile approach to the Soviet Union, and it still bears the nasty aftertaste of the McCarthyite witch-hunts. It has, moreover, usually been applied in a top-heavy and static manner. That is, it has over-emphasised political control mechanisms, giving the impression that society was mere malleable putty in the hands of the ruling party. And it has proved ill equipped to explain, still less predict, change: those who use it have on the whole assumed that, once in place, the totalitarian polity is permanent, not susceptible to the processes of internal evolution which affect most political systems. Richard Pipes, for instance, has asserted that it is 'by definition incapable of evolution from within and impervious to change from without'.[14]

As it stands, this statement is plainly wrong, but its partial blindness harbours an important element of insight. Totalitarian systems *are* quite unusually rigid, as Gorbachev is discovering to his cost. But nowadays we have enough information about the lower levels of Soviet society;

and we can look back on a time-span sufficient for gradual change to be obvious. Nor are we unduly influenced by cold war sentiment any more. So there is no reason why we should perpetuate the obvious deficiencies of the model, which have led so many scholars to reject it altogether.

For a totalitarian society is neither demonic, nor unchanging, nor totally manipulated from above. Actually, it is 'human, all too human'. If we can rehumanise our understanding of it, see it in its historical context, and reawaken our sense of how the various social strata, nationalities and religions operate and interact under it, then I believe the totalitarian model is capable of affording us a more complete view of Soviet society than any alternative yet propounded. Indeed, it provides the most satisfactory explanation of the processes which have generated the country's current crisis, as well as making it clear why thorough-going reform (or as Gorbachev prefers to call it, 'restructuring': *perestroika*) is so extraordinarily difficult to bring off. 'Stagnation' is a logical result (though not the only possible result) of Lenin's revolution of 1917. His determination to pursue his utopian vision alone, even in the face of opposition from the other socialist parties, to risk civil war rather than enter coalitions and agreements which would require him to compromise any of his programme, led naturally to a political monopoly which, given the technical accomplishments of the twentieth century, assumed unprecedented proportions.

So I make no apologies for resurrecting the notion of 'totalitarianism'. I believe that it enables us to understand both why radical reform has become so urgently necessary, and also why it is proving so difficult to carry out. Remove the term 'totalitarian', and it is not obvious how the Soviet Union differs from, say, Spain under Franco or Chile under Pinochet. But these differences are crucial.

Until Gorbachev's perestroika began to take hold, the Soviet Union was a society marked by three decisive features. Its political life was entirely monopolised by one body, the Communist Party, which dominated organisationally all governmental and public institutions, and governed appointments to all responsible jobs through the *nomenklatura* system. The party's ideology was the only permitted intellectual system, and it was projected to the population using all the resources of the media, culture and the educational system. Its economy was wholly directed from the centre (with the sole exception of the peasant garden plots), and everybody was directly or indirectly an employee of the state.

Of course this system functioned in a different way under Brezhnev than it had under Stalin. Institutionally, perhaps the most significant change was that the security police had been brought under party control and could no longer apply indiscriminate terror against the party itself under the direction of a single dictator. Correspondingly the arbitrary power of the leader diminished and became diffused among an oligarchy at the apex of the party-state apparatus. Underneath, too, radical social change was taking place in a way which pointed towards eventual political reform, but was not enough in itself to shake the tough framework of the system.

The first and perhaps most important feature of the totalitarian polity is that it produced a nation traumatised by its own past. It is difficult for us to grasp the sheer scale of the human suffering involved, but we know that, according to recent Soviet estimates, the mass collectivisation of agriculture in the thirties subjected ten to fifteen million peasants to forcible expropriation and deportation.[15] We know that a substantial proportion died, many of them in the ensuing famine. Moreover, from about the mid-thirties to the mid-fifties, millions of Soviet citizens were in slave labour camps, where the death rate may have been 10 per cent a year. Some historians believe the victims of Stalin's brutality may well have outnumbered the twenty million usually cited by Soviet sources as the figure for those killed in the Second World War.[16]

And this is not to mention the tens of millions uprooted from their homes by less abnormal social processes, like industrialisation and military service. When Boris Pasternak wrote his *Essay in Autobiography*, he broke off before this period with the words: 'To continue would be immeasurably difficult . . . One would have to write in such a way as to make the hair stand on end and the heart falter.'[17]

I myself have found over the years that, as I get to know Soviet citizens of the middle and older generations, I discover that all of them have been scarred in one way or another by that terrible epoch. One will remember being deported in a cattle truck to Siberia; another that, when he was six, his father simply disappeared and was never heard of again; another recalls standing with her mother in long queues outside prisons, waiting to deliver food parcels and hoping for a scrap of information about her father. Those who were in labour camps and came out alive are usually very reluctant to talk about the experience, perhaps agreeing with Varlam Shalamov, survivor of Kolyma, that 'the camps were a negative school of life in every respect . . . There was much there that no man should know or see, or, if he has seen it, it is better he should die.'[18]

Shalamov, fortunately, did not follow his own precept: he chronicled his labour camp experience in a series of gritty, icily factual stories.[19] But most Soviet people have preferred not to dwell too much on the grim past. Now when a nation cannot face its own past, it will have difficulty with its future too. We have seen something of this in German society since the war, but the effect is far deeper in the Soviet Union, for there the regime responsible for the trauma is still in place, and till very recently it had only feebly and indecisively denounced its own crimes. A whole nation has been unable properly to mourn its murdered and tormented. This theme of the belated and halting recovery of memory is one to which I shall return, for it helps to explain the travail in which Soviet society is rebuilding its civic consciousness.

Another crucial feature which distinguishes the totalitarian regime from the merely authoritarian is that it has created its own society. Whereas Franco and Pinochet (and arguably even Hitler) inherited social structures from the past and sought by and large to preserve them, the Communist Party began its rule by destroying an old society and creating a new one in its own image. The new ruling class was delineated by the *nomenklatura* system, set up in the early twenties, through which party committees began to keep regularly updated files on all individuals whom they regarded as potentially suitable for nomination to public office. Since a party recommendation is crucial to any appointment, in this way the party Central Committee directly or indirectly controls the patronage of all responsible posts in Soviet society, including those which are in principle elective. All other social classes – and, for that matter, nationalities – fall into place in a hierarchical pyramid whose framework the party has constructed. It is true that with time these raw social classes have gradually acquired their own way of life, their traditions and customs, but the party is integrally woven into these as the guiding and directing institution.

That basic fact governs the next major distinct characteristic of the totalitarian system: its unique pervasiveness. The Communist Party not only leads and guides society, it penetrates it. It has its cells in every factory, farm, office, school, and block of flats. It unceasingly supervises, indoctrinates, exhorts, and mobilises – not always successfully, it is true, but its presence is invariably evident. Through the *nomenklatura* network, it has a grip on patronage in every social hierarchy. It watches over the economy and sorts out the muddles and bottlenecks which inevitably arise when the planning system gets tangled in its own tentacles. It socialises the people through the education system. It speaks to the people through the mass media. It preaches to the people through its propagandists and agitators. It both claims and exercises an exclusive right to all these forms of authority, a prerogative bestowed upon it by history, of which its guardians profess a superior understanding.

Since this right to rule rests on ideology, it follows that totalitarianism is a system which attributes paramount importance to ideas. The ideas may be debased, but they are everywhere. Every student, whatever his subject of study, has to pass examinations in Political Economy, Dialectical Materialism, Scientific Atheism, and the like. The acquaintances of my student days at Moscow University used to say they were bored silly by these subjects: they would knit or write letters during the lectures, and then desperately mug up the material out of a textbook the night before the exam. One might think that studies pursued in this way could hardly have a profound effect, but in fact I feel that the impact of all this ideological cramming is not altogether superficial.

Rote-learning has a way of clinging to odd corners of the mind, and turning up unexpectedly, maybe years later. In any case, the effect is constantly being reinforced by the ever present slogans on street banners, wall-posters, in the newspapers, and on radio and television. As the émigré novelist Aleksandr Zinoviev puts it, Soviet citizens are 'in constant contact with the powerful magnetic field of ideological influence . . . They absorb from it a certain electrical charge . . . There is physically no way they can escape from it'.[20] This, of course, is especially true for the literate, for those who live in towns, and those who perform administrative or intellectual work, that is, the fastest-growing sector of the population.

This all-pervading ideological 'static' does not necessarily make everyone a Marxist-Leninist zombie. Far from it. But it does inculcate in the average Soviet citizen the habit of systematic, monological thinking on social, political and philosophical issues, an inclination which remains with him even if he disavows the official ideology. The instinct for seeing problems as a whole, and taking up vehement, unambiguous stances on them, has permeated the gradual revival of civic consciousness in the Soviet Union, as we shall see.

Another paradoxical fruit of the ascendancy of ideology is that it confers high social status on people whose profession is ideas. In the west such people often have to seek niches in jobs where ideas are a by-product. In the Soviet Union, by contrast, the purveyors of ideas are more independent of day-to-day utilitarian pressures: they can work in the party's huge ideological apparatus of instructors, propagandists and agitators. They can go to ground in one of the many research institutes maintained by the party, the government or the Academy of Sciences, none of which ever see anything so demanding as a student wishing to be taught. They can join one of the creative unions, such as the Union of Writers, which exists to free authors from the need to support themselves by mercenary drudgery (ironically, many of them in consequence produce their own species of dreary hackwork, but then that itself is a tribute to the respect accorded even to derivative ideas).

In short, there exists in Soviet society a certain confidence that ideas, especially all-embracing, systematic ideas, are worthy of respect as such and require no extrinsic justification. Given the normal human propensity to discern charm in forbidden fruit, this confidence bestows on alternative, non-Marxist intellectual, cultural and philosophical systems a considerable creative, or should one say subversive, potential.

Last among the key distinctive features of the totalitarian society is the unusual depth of the divide it opens up in the individual between the public and the private persona. To some extent we are all familiar with this divide. No one in any society behaves towards his employer exactly as he would with a close friend. But nowhere is the split so radical as under totalitarian rule. Most people, whatever their private views, cultivate in public a façade of conformity and anonymity: they do what is expected of them. 'A meeting', in the apt definition coined by the satirical novelist Vladimir Voinovich, 'is an occasion when people gather together, some to say what they do not think, and others not to say what they really do.'[21]

This institutionally induced doublethink engenders what appears on the surface to be an almost limitless flexibility of outlook. People's opinions change, or seem to, with the same abruptness as the party line. How many unexpected 'liberals' did the advent of glasnost not suddenly reveal! Editors and critics who had not stinted in their paeans to what later became known as 'the era of stagnation' were transformed overnight into convinced exponents of perestroika. Which of the two they really believe remains an enigma. We should not take too seriously, then, what passes in the Soviet media for 'public opinion'.

As against the impressive but brittle unanimity of public life, Soviet citizens cultivate their private pursuits and attachments with an intensity seldom seen in more relaxed societies. Behind the carefully contrived façade of anonymity and conformity, they discreetly 'do their own thing' in the company of like-minded individuals. That 'thing' can vary from rock music to abstract art to the discussion of Hegelian philosophy to Yogic meditation. What such groups have in common is that they are dealing in cultural artefacts and ideas. Many of them have turned, naturally enough, to their own semi-suppressed national traditions, whether Russian or non-Russian. As an occasional privileged interloper in such gatherings over the last quarter of a century, I can testify to their remarkable warmth, humanity and spiritual intensity. This is the milieu in which the political anecdote flourishes – that backhanded tribute of oppressed intellectuals to the rulers who subjugate them. It is also a milieu in which the exchange and exploration of ideas proceeds with utter spontaneity and at the same time concentration. In my experience, the art of conversation is pursued in Moscow at a higher level than anywhere else in the world.

Until recently, one could have stated confidently that this intellectual ferment produced little discernible social result. It remained perforce essentially private. It is true that the movement called 'dissent' grew out of it. 'Dissidents' were people of this kind, forced to 'go public' because the state had invaded their private domain, charging them and their colleagues with 'anti-Soviet propaganda' for circulating among themselves thoughts not admitted to the official canon. Nearly all westerners misinterpreted dissent, in a classical example of the failure to see the whole Soviet context. They took it for a political movement aiming to bring about political change, and accordingly judged it a failure. Actually it was the mere dislocated tip of an iceberg, whose depths harboured a powerful reaffirmation of personal identity and community – a spiritual not a political movement. Judged in its own terms it was not a failure but a remarkable success, and ultimately it has brought forth political fruits as well, in the diverse and beneficial flowering of glasnost, which is otherwise impossible to explain.

Elements of pluralism do emerge, then, at least potentially, under the totalitarian carapace. But they are very different from the competing interest groups with which we are familiar in western societies. They are formed on the basis not of material interests, but of culture and ideas, in keeping with the society to which they belong. They do not compete in an open forum for media attention or for influence on the electoral process. On the contrary, until recently they have deliberately shunned all publicity, seeking it, if at all, only when the state violates their fragile boundaries. The Soviet Union has been a deeply segmented society, in which a multitude of diverse associations existed, but did not interact with one another. Nowadays they are beginning to, generating the 'turmoil' which is normal politics, but which so disconcerts Mr Gorbachev's colleagues.

All of which brings me back to Disgusted Sverdlovsk. The crisis he is witnessing is the crisis of Soviet totalitarianism. The system is undermining itself through its own inherent contradictions, putting at risk the great power status which that system once achieved.

From the leadership's viewpoint, the totalitarian pathology is most evident and damaging in the economy. The decision to set up centrally administered planning under Stalin was fateful, for it delivered the economy into the hands of a ruling class of a historically unprecedented kind. Founded by Lenin and brought to perfection by Stalin, this ruling class has both its anchor and its forum in the party Central Committee. Its origins go back to the years during and after the civil war, when the Bolsheviks were tightening their at first precarious grip on a country in deep turmoil. Lenin's 'professional revolutionaries' were becoming professional administrators (or, if they proved unsuited to this new role, were being replaced by Stalin's nominees), responsible for a huge country in extreme disorder and poverty. Their methods of rule were not the traditional ones. They infiltrated the structures of power as well as dominating them from above. The party rules published in December 1919 laid down that wherever there were three or more party members in any organisation, it was their duty to form a party cell 'whose task it is to increase party influence in every direction, carry out party policies in non-party milieux, and effect party supervision over the work of all organisations and institutions'.[22]

One of the ways in which the party cell carried out this instruction was by keeping lists of employees in all organisations, and especially of people suitable, from the party's point of view, for promotion. The 'great and the good', as it were. These lists were passed up the party ladder and, under Stalin as General Secretary from 1922, they were extended, systematised and kept up to date. Not for nothing did Stalin's comrades dub him 'Comrade Card Index'.

Those who had lived through revolution and civil war tended to assume that, as Mao Zedong later put it, 'power grows out of the barrel of a gun'. It took them a long time to realise that, on the contrary, in a one-party system where the state soon became the sole employer, power was henceforth to proceed from the filing cabinet. Stalin's personnel lists became the instrument of the *nomenklatura* system, under which every single appointment to any responsible job, in whatever walk of life, was decided only after approval by a party committee at the appropriate level. The committee would make its nomination only on the basis of reports filed and kept up to date by the potential appointee's previous employers, by his trade union committee, by his party organisation, and by the security police. Thus was constituted an all-embracing network of information and patronage without equal in any previous society.[23]

It was buttressed by a panoply of honours and privileges. Since responsible office-holders could not be expected to tolerate the wretched conditions in which most Soviet citizens lived, they were granted access to more spacious housing, superior medical care and special stores with cheap, good quality food. As it developed, the ladder of privilege became minutely graded according to the ranking of one's post in the *nomenklatura* hierarchy: those at the very top would receive the best apartments, doctors and groceries, and in addition might qualify for a country dacha, a chauffeur-driven car and a holiday abroad.

The *nomenklatura* hierarchy is, then, one not just of power and patronage, but also of material interests. Money and inheritance, as they operate in most societies, are replaced by privilege and political clientelism. The result is an unprecedentedly monolithic and dominant ruling class.

Of course, some things have changed since Stalin's death, but not in such a way as to endanger the grip which the *nomenklatura* office-holders have on society. On the contrary. Stalin may have created them, but they can exist very well without him. Better in fact than under him. While he was alive, they flourished as a class, but individually they had to tremble for their positions and indeed their lives. Since his death the party Central Committee (which we may think of as the *nomenklatura* 'inner circle') has brought his murderous security police firmly under control. Under Brezhnev's slogan of 'stability of cadres' the *nomenklatura* appointees have been able to regard their posts as virtually lifetime incumbencies. Benefiting from corruption, personal acquaintances and their own subordinate patronage, they have consolidated their position by dispensing favours downwards to selected recipients, while using the police, the procuracy and the law courts to stifle their opponents. If you like, 'stability of cadres' was the 'little Stalins' charter'.

The planned economy is the principal arena in which these office-holders have deployed their power, and from it they derive their generous emoluments. It is both their *raison d'être* and their feeding trough. The Soviet economy is in effect a huge institutionalised sellers' market, run for the benefit of those who operate it, not of those who have to use its products. It flourishes on grandiose projects – which increase the scope of patronage – but cannot respond to the highly differentiated demands of today's consumers. It actually penalises both innovation and high quality work, the driving forces which are needed to ensure for the Soviet Union an economic base appropriate to a twenty-first-century great power.

The resulting milieu of low pay and permanent underproduction is the familiar home of the great majority of Soviet citizens – those, that is, who do not have access to privileges assigned from above. Prices of housing, transport and basic foodstuffs are relatively low, and the authorities prefer to keep it that way. When Khrushchev raised meat prices in the early sixties there was rioting in the streets, and the leaders are regularly reminded by developments in neighbouring Poland how defiant workers can become when asked to pay more for their food. To fulfil this side of their tacit social contract with the workforce, the Soviet state pays out the equivalent of some fifty billion dollars a year in subsidies.[24]

Of course, cheap commodities in short supply have to be rationed somehow, and in the Soviet Union they are rationed by the queue. Most Soviet citizens expect to spend part of the day standing in line along with hundreds of their surly, frustrated fellow-citizens. They tend, indeed, to regard the right to do this during working hours as another aspect of that tacit 'social contract': 'They pretend to pay us, and we pretend to work.' In order to keep the queuing down to a minimum, though, most of them also devise at least some private arrangements, through bribery, or personal acquaintance, or mutual favours, to obtain the supplies or services of which they have most regular need. Thus a shop assistant may keep back a good cut of meat in return for a tip, or a garage mechanic may perform motor repairs for imported clothing. The permutations are endless, but they nearly always involve time, tools or goods diverted from the official economy. The 'second economy' is essential to a tolerable life, but it is also parasitic on the official one and therefore dependent upon it. Its devices are precarious, and both seller and customer have an interest in their remaining undisturbed.

This situation gives most Soviet citizens a certain stake in the status quo. They cannot afford to have their private arrangements disrupted unless successful reform of the entire economy follows, so that goods and services hitherto obtainable only clandestinely become regularly available at affordable prices. Much of the unease provoked by Gorbachev's measures derives from the fear that in his drive against corruption he will upset existing contrivances without putting stable patterns of supply in their place.

It is not, then, only the *nomenklatura* élite who have an interest in the prevailing system. To some extent most people have become dependent on it, or have at least sought out a tolerable niche within it which is vulnerable to the winds of perestroika.

Yet the system inspires only a limited and conditional loyalty. For in other ways it engenders evils which people are well aware of and find extremely irksome, even oppressive. The general squalor and neglect, the confined intellectual life, the cultural censorship, the religious restrictions, the obstacles to foreign travel, the bureaucratic obstruction- ism, the degradation of the environment: all these deficiencies are perceived by most Soviet citizens as products of the system and as serious impediments to what they nostalgically like to call 'normal life'. And that includes a lot of members of the élite. To eliminate these evils, or even some of them, most people would be prepared, in my experience, to support an out-and-out reformer, if only they could be sure that their present precarious sufficiency would not be destroyed without anything more lasting and satisfactory being substituted. For that reason, the natural reaction to a reforming leader is initial caution, even inert resistance. But this could give way to enthusiastic support if he is seen to be succeeding. In most people's eyes, however, Gorbachev has not yet made the vital breakthrough. That is one major source of his difficulties.

Another is that his reform programme entails a crucial paradox. A serious loosening of the economy, let alone of politics and intellectual life, will dislocate the mainspring of the power which the Communist Party's full time officials, the *apparatchiki*, have arrogated to themselves. They are well aware of the fact. To be fair to them, some party secretaries also recognise the seriousness of the present crisis, and the need for drastic remedies, at least to judge by their speeches at the 19th Party Conference in the summer of 1988. But the bulk of the medium and lower level *apparatchiks*, who are perhaps less well informed and certainly have narrower perspectives, are resentful at any prospect of losing their grip on power and privilege. And they can still claim the mandate of history in support of their prejudices.

So do the reformers stand a chance, or are their efforts doomed to failure? To a considerable extent, the answer depends not on them, but on the response of Soviet society. We in the west tend to write Russians off as passive, even slavish, and to assume that, because they have no native tradition of democracy, they are incapable of ever creating a more open and pluralist polity.

There is, of course, something in this: Russians do not have a heritage of democracy as we understand that term. All the same, I do not believe they are condemned to eternal civic passivity. On the contrary, I believe that they have derived, from their past, traditions of political participation and mutual solidarity under pressure which are proving to be decisive elements in the new situation, and which are creating the makings of a civil society.

2

Communities and ideals
in Russian society

Visiting the Soviet Union today, one is tempted at times to believe that Russia's past has disappeared entirely. Standing in a modern Soviet street, I sometimes feel as if I were in a society afflicted by communal amnesia, disoriented like an alcoholic who wakes to discover he can't remember what happened the day before. The town may be old, but it now bears a brand new name, that of some Soviet hero, and the gigantic architectural monoliths in which most Soviet citizens live have obliterated all traces of previous settlement, of ancient fields and pathways. It does not seem possible in the Soviet *tabula rasa* that any form of social institution or even memory can have survived revolutions, wars, purges and forced industrialisation to offer a foothold for a more pluralist mode of politics today.

At the start of my career I studied the State Duma, the short-lived parliament of tsarist Russia's last years. The Duma had serious powers, it contained a variety of political parties, and it debated the issues of the day in an unconstrained and well-informed manner. At its birth the British House of Commons sent it a telegram welcoming it to the international family of parliaments. Perhaps there, I thought, one might find a thread from the past, the first rudiments of a democratic tradition. But I soon discovered that today's Soviet intellectuals, even those with a concern for freedom, are not reading the ideas of Milyukov or Guchkov, who were the two leading liberal members of that assembly.

While I was in Moscow, I did, though, discover something else, something which pointed to at least some kind of inherited sense of community. Take the following scene, which I believe will be familiar to most people who have spent some time in the Soviet Union. You have been invited to a friend's home one evening. You want to take a little present, so you trudge round the shops looking for something – a box of chocolates, flowers, even just some decent sausage meat. But the shelves are empty and the salesgirls sullenly unhelpful. Tired and discouraged, you struggle on to a crowded bus where all the other passengers have oversized elbows and feet. Getting off again, you tramp through the freezing air, and make your way into the filthy, evil-smelling vestibule of a block of flats.

Then you ring at the doorbell . . . and a magic transformation takes place. Your friends welcome you. Whether or not you have managed to bring a contribution, you are seated in front of a feast which may be modest but must have taken hours of ingenuity to assemble. The vodka – or in the Gorbachev era, the tea – begins to circulate. You plunge into discussion of literature, philosophy, science, politics – everything under the sun. You feel for a while – and is it an illusion? – that you are part of a warm human community talking about the things which really matter in life.

This is, I believe, the archetypal Russian experience, and it goes far back into history. A freezing climate, squalid externals, a harsh and inadequate official system contrast with a warm interior, a humane and cultured personal life. If we are to understand Russians at all, we have to take this dichotomy into account. It is both geographically and histor-ically determined. In order to hold their vast, frozen territories together, and on the basis of them to claim the status of an international great power, Russian governments over the centuries have had to extract the maximum resources from a scattered and poverty-stricken population. From the time of Peter the Great in the early eighteenth century, and arguably earlier as well, Russian governments have endeavoured to create institutions which would make it possible to raise and maintain a huge army, to create industry backed by modern science and tech-nology, and generally to mobilise the population for the tasks incumbent upon a great power. The remarkable thing is that they have succeeded to a considerable extent, but usually in ways that have something of the *trompe l'œil* about them, and that leave Russians themselves feeling surprisingly vulnerable.

Institutions in Russia never function quite as intended by the government that set them up. There are a number of good reasons for this: immense distances, harsh climate, economic and cultural backwardness (compared with the western models on which Russian institutions are usually designed), and the inadequate provision of resources by the government itself. Instead, institutions take on a life of their own, determined by the needs of the human beings who actually man them. These needs do not necessarily coincide with the purposes of the government, and may indeed run directly counter to them. Hence the feeling the historian has, when reading the papers of Russian statesmen, that they are wearily doing their best, with their impeccable juridical phraseology, to grasp a reality which constantly eludes them. At the grass roots, people improvise a façade for the occasional appearance of the dreaded 'government inspector', but otherwise do their own thing in their own way, treating officials as just another unpredictable element in a forbidding environment.

This cardinal characteristic of Russian society has always been difficult for historians or social scientists to grasp. For we are largely dependent on documents, and documents come on the whole from governments, not from the grass roots, where indeed people may actually be anxious to *conceal* the reality of what they are doing. So we write history from above, and marvel that Russians have been able to survive at all the asperities of their climate and their political system, not to mention repeated foreign invasions.

But they *have* survived, battered, bruised and intimidated though they may be. Indeed, in some respects, they have flourished, as one realises if one looks at the best of their culture, science and learning, which are on the highest international level. I believe, in fact, that the Russian people have demonstrated an extraordinary capacity to improvise humane and functioning grass roots institutions in extremely could do much to simplify the arrival in a city of a peasant looking for lodging and work. When in the 1890s Semyon Kanatchikov was brought as a teenager into Moscow by his father to seek employment, his path was smoothed in this way. 'We rented an apartment communally, as an *artel'* of about fifteen men. Some were bachelors, others had wives who lived in the village and ran their households . . . Our food and the woman who prepared it were also paid for communally. The food was purchased on credit at a shop; our individual shares were assessed twice monthly.'[5]

Of course, we must be quite clear what kind of institutions the *mir* and *artel'* were. They displayed no democracy or civil freedom in the western sense. They encouraged no concept of citizenship, individual ownership or individual rights. The predominant force in them was not the rule of law, but that of custom and authority. Nevertheless, as human communities operating in a grim and oppressive environment, they had much to commend them. They certainly afforded security and a means of getting things done. Moreover, even in this relatively primitive form, they have not entirely disappeared. As every foreign student at a Soviet university knows, he and his co-nationals will be expected to form a cohesive group and elect a *starosta* who will conduct all their dealings with the authorities. Any other method of getting things done will be met not just with disapproval, but with incomprehension.

If, then, we want to understand the Russian revolution and the Soviet state, it is very important to bear in mind that they sprang from this capacity of the Russian people for improvising grass roots institutions in circumstances of difficulty or emergency. In my view, the dogged radicalism of Russian workers and peasants in 1917 derived not from Marxism, but from the unusually late survival into the industrial world of popular institutions of primitive solidarity, accustomed to steering round governments, offering their officials passive resistance or profiting by their inadequacies.

Take, for example, the institution of the soviet, which gives the Union of Soviet Socialist Republics its present name. It first arose in the textile city of Ivanovo-Voznesensk, when a general strike was called there in May 1905. Delegates from the various mills gathered on the banks of the River Talka: they were the men whom the workers had chosen to represent them on the so-called Shidlovskii Commission, set up by the government to examine possible industrial legislation. Now, consulting on the river bank, in a position where they were challenging both employers and government, these delegates decided to put their representative functions to a completely new use, that is, to represent their fellows in negotiations with both employers and government, and in the meanwhile to improvise minimal services for a city in which the normal administrative bodies were paralysed.[6]

So a completely new institution was born, the Soviet of Workers' Deputies, embryo of the present-day Soviet state. It acted at one and the same time as strike committee and temporary local government assembly. It was elected by the workers of the various mills, any of whom had the right to attend its debates. Delegates could be recalled at any time, if their electors disapproved of what they were doing, and replaced by others. Outside the market square of Athens it was perhaps the closest approach to direct democracy that can be conceived.

The idea caught on fast. During the next few months similar soviets sprang up all over Russia, the most famous of which, the St Petersburg Soviet, paralysed the capital city in October, and pressured the tsar into promising civil freedoms and the establishment of a national legislative assembly. And when the tsarist regime fell in March 1917, the first thought of workers all over Russia was to rush to form soviets of the kind they had briefly experienced in 1905.

If one believes the commonly accepted picture of Russian workers as politically unformed, then this rapid spread of effective political institutions is difficult to explain. Some of course would attribute it to the skill and vigour of the revolutionary parties, and there is unquestionably something in this. Both the Social Democrats and the Socialist Revolutionaries offered cogent explanations of the workers' discontents, and an inspiring mandate for action. But most accounts, even from the revolutionaries themselves, agree that the socialist politicians were taken aback by the swiftness with which the workers improvised their own organisations. Lenin, in particular, initially viewed the soviets with grave misgivings, though he later changed his mind in view of their obvious effectiveness.

No, I believe the relative success of the soviets in 1905 and 1917 was chiefly due to the long experience of both peasants and workers in creating and running their own grass roots institutions, an experience long ago lost in more advanced countries where the environment was less harsh, the economy more productive and the government more effective.

In the villages of 1917 the peasants displayed a similar capacity for collective action. With the breakdown of law and order – or at least of the law and order imposed by church, police and landowner – they saw their chance to assert their own conception of how affairs should be run. The natural place for them to meet, discuss the situation, and take decisions was the *skhod*, the communal assembly. And there they would often come to the conclusion that an opportune time had come for them to rectify age-old injustices, by invading the landowner's land and taking his timber, pasturing village cattle on his fields, harvesting his crops, or even driving him out and burning down his manor house so that he could not easily return. Having reached such a resolution, they would implement it as a body, sharing the responsibility and the risks. They would sound the *nabat*, or alarm bell, gather with their carts, and troop together up to the manor house, to demand from the bailiff the keys to the barns and store-sheds, and then, provided there was no resistance, they would escort the squire and his family courteously off the premises.

The village commune had in other words its own conception of law and order, which it endeavoured to put into practice. Maverick fellow villagers who tried to grab more than their fair share, or who looted the squire's liquor supply for their own consumption, were treated as criminals by the community.[7]

In short, then, in the freedom, but also dangers, of 1917, peasants and workers reacted by improvising their own institutions, such as would enable them to take advantage of opportunities offered, and to defend themselves against threats. They drew in the revolutionary parties to help and advise them, where possible. But they did not always accept their advice, and where such help was not forthcoming, went ahead anyway.

The Bolsheviks came to power in October not least because they were the party best attuned to the mood in these popular institutions. They sponsored the popular demands for bread, land, workers' control in the factories, and an end to the war. Most of the workers, soldiers and peasants who supported the Bolshevik seizure of power in October thought they were fighting for 'All Power to the Soviets', as Lenin's slogan put it.[8]

In reality, of course, things turned out differently. The soviets and their equivalents held effective power only for a few months at most under the Bolshevik government. Then the pressures of economic collapse, civil war and the ingrained authoritarianism of Lenin brought a steady tightening of central control over all popular institutions. Instead of being elected, their officials came to be appointed from above. Rival political parties were gradually squeezed out, and then even alternative platforms within the Bolshevik party were banned, rendering genuine political debate more and more difficult. The Bolsheviks proved far more competent than the tsarist government at asserting effective control over the grass roots. They were better organised, more ruthless, had a far more developed sense of propaganda and mobilis-ation. Besides, many younger peasants and workers from poorer families – the very ones who had found the old village commune stifling – were thoroughly committed to the new regime, and were prepared to act as its devoted agents through thick and thin. They formed the indispensable base of social support for the new one-party state and the totalitarian system which it erected.[9]

Having sponsored and led this revolution of workers' and peasants' communities, the Communist Party later also destroyed them, partly in the civil war, partly a decade later in the whirlwind collectivisation of agriculture. The soviets of town and country became mere instruments of one-party domination.

It is my impression, though, that even after these popular

communities were destroyed, something of their *spirit* survived in distorted form in the dwelling patterns of the city, in the so-called 'communal apartments', where for decades families lived squeezed next to one another owing to the desperate housing shortage. There, in shared poverty, they had perforce to devise a consensus about the common use of kitchen and bathroom, and they kept an even closer eye on one another than was possible in the village. Even today, when the communal apartment is no longer universal, the basic unit of Soviet urban life, the large block of flats grouped round a courtyard, still has something rural about it. The men sit at table and play cards or dominoes, the women gather and exchange gossip, the children amuse themselves in the sandpits. Such scenes can be found in Moscow as much as in smaller towns, and are very different from the texture of urban life in most of Europe.

Nor is it just a matter of dwelling patterns. The underlying habit of mutual aid, combined with mutual supervision, has survived and indeed spread to other strata of the population as former peasant children left the village and moved up the social scale. The very speed of the urbanisation process, reinforced by the absence of pluralist political institutions in the towns, may actually have artificially preserved elements of rural culture inside the urban environment. In this way the totalitarian polity may have accidentally perpetuated an archaic communal outlook that would otherwise have faded more rapidly.[10]

I believe, in fact, that attitudes derived from the village have permeated the middle and lower levels of the Soviet political and economic systems, and still make themselves felt today. They should help us to understand how the totalitarian system works in practice. Since absolute control from the top is impossible, even the totalitarian state has to transmit its commands through intermediate institutions, and these tend gradually to evolve their own forms of internal solidarity. In his classical study of Soviet politics, written in the 1950s, the American political scientist Merle Fainsod hypothesised that totalitarianism tends to engender its own antibodies, even within the apparatus of power itself. 'Faced with demands from the party leadership which are difficult if not impossible to fulfil, and confronted with the constant possibility of a crossfire of criticisms from many directions, party as well as governmental functionaries are tempted to seek a degree of independence from control by organising mutual protection associations in which they agree informally to refrain from mutual criticism and to cover up for each other's mistakes and deficiencies.'[11]

In this way transmission belts can also become islands of resistance, indeed a whole network of resistance which eventually clogs up the system. This is entirely in keeping with the ambivalent Russian spirit of community: the peasant *mir* served both as the lowest rung in the ladder of authoritarian control, and yet also as a means by which ordinary people could cushion themselves against the excessive demands of the state. I suspect the same applies to Fainsod's 'mutual protection associations' and indeed to many grass roots Soviet institutions. In his study of industrial managers, Joseph Berliner calls them 'family circles', which well catches the analogy with rural congeries.[12]

So far westerners have not had the experience and Soviet scholars have not had the theoretical insight to write systematically about institutions at the lowest level. As a result, we know very little about the way village soviets, collective farm meetings, house committees and so on operate. The only observer who has attempted an extensive survey of the grass roots is Alexander Zinoviev, the philosopher who emigrated in 1977 at the age of 54, and has expatiated on his experience in a series of monographs in semi-fictional, semi-scientific form. He sees Soviet society as a network of tightly knit primary cells, centred at the workplace, which he calls 'communes'. In his presentation they sound like degenerate extended peasant households, held together by a web of material dependence, servility towards superiors, and mutual support adulterated by mutual jealousy and supervision.

These are the basic features of what Zinoviev calls 'communality', which he holds to be a universal human trait, restrained in most societies, but given free rein by Communism. Their inescapable result, as he sees it, is 'a tendency to make everyone mediocre. Be like everyone else: that principle is the very cornerstone of a society in which communal laws are paramount.'[13] Of course, one must remember that Zinoviev's vantage point is that of a highly talented intellectual who had been trying to publish unorthodox works. He naturally therefore emphasises the levelling effects of the primary cells. But there is no doubt in any case that Russian communities have always tended to crush or extrude their eccentrics, even (or especially) those who were talented, since divergences from the collective norms always seemed hazardous to a community on the edge of survival. As Zinoviev sees it:

'A person who can live in society independently of a primary collective is a threat to the very foundations of society. He is like a soldier who doesn't march in step with the rest of the platoon, but wanders about at random independently of the rest. He annoys the rest.'[14]

These 'communes' are the most important units of Soviet society, and their attitudes shape all the others, including families, circles of friends, even official institutions. This is because they dispense to each individual the basic ingredients of material and social life, including simple sociability, many of which are otherwise difficult to secure at all in Soviet society.

'At the level of the primary collective people not only work, they spend their time in the company of people they know well. They swap news, amuse themselves, do all kinds of things to preserve and improve their position, have contact with people on whom their well-being depends, go to innumerable meetings, get sent on leave to rest-homes, are assigned accommodation and sometimes supplementary food-products.'[15]

These are the daily confines of Soviet society, and in Zinoviev's opinion they render control from above superfluous. (For that reason, he rejects the term 'totalitarian', but we are not obliged to follow him: in any case, he clearly considers the hierarchical context within which the 'communes' operate to be crucial.) On their own they suffice to explain the homogeneity and conformism of *Homo sovieticus*. The security police is no more than the concentrated quintessence of society's outlook, usually superfluous since the communes will spontaneously eject their own mavericks and dissenters.

Zinoviev is perhaps unaware of the cultural limitations of his view.

The kind of 'communality' he describes is not necessarily characteristic of humanity everywhere. But it may well be characteristic of many peasant societies, and its prevalence in Russia may be explained by the fact that the pre-modern peasant community survived there till more recently, and in harsher circumstances, than in most European countries.

I believe that, for all its limitations, Zinoviev's loquacious analysis opens up significant insights. He offers us what Philip Hanson has aptly called 'totalitarianism from below'.[16] If we want to understand how change can come about from below in such a society, then this is the unit from which we must start. However, as I said in the first chapter, the bearers of change in totalitarian society are intellectuals, so we must consider how these 'communes' function among them.

The Communist Party, which first supported, then took over and finally emasculated the popular assemblies, grew from the ranks of the radical intelligentsia, whose ideas and whose forms of community life are therefore of fundamental importance in understanding the influences which have shaped Soviet society.

The intelligentsia were the bastard children of Peter the Great, who in the early eighteenth century set out to make primitive Muscovy into a great European power. He succeeded, despite the enormity of the task, by using the power of the monarchy to transform all Russia's social institutions. In particular, he made the landed nobility into state servitors of army and bureaucracy, and he moulded the Church into an instrument for education, social welfare and the supervision of the common people. In the process, he laid the foundation for a tradition of public service which was one of the most attractive and abiding features of Imperial Russian society. But he also gravely weakened both the nobility and the clergy, depriving them of the autonomy which enabled them, in most European societies, to make their own distinctive input into the political process.

This enthralment was particularly damaging to the clergy, especially the parish clergy, who in the course of the eighteenth and nineteenth centuries became a subordinate estate, in effect almost an inferior caste, bereft of the financial provision, institutional independence or social standing which an established church normally enjoys.[17] Even the anti-clerical French republic of the late nineteenth century did not treat its clergy so shabbily. Yet the tsar still claimed to rule by divine right: this was expressly stated in the Fundamental Laws. The legitimacy of the Russian state, and therefore its symbolism, were religious, but its aims and methods were secular. It humiliated the very institution on whose sanction it rested its authority.

This fundamental incongruity created fertile soil for a revolutionary movement. Russia's revolutionaries came mainly from the two estates – nobility and clergy – which also provided its state servants. A study of the biographies of revolutionaries of the 1860s and '70s shows that they through their formative experiences at educational establishments – universities, colleges and seminaries – designed to train them for public service. There, however, many of them came to the conclusion that the existing state and church were too corrupt and degraded to fulfil their proper function. Some students thereupon switched their allegiance to the revolutionary movement in the hope that it could do what state and church could not: genuinely serve the people.[18]

What had the revolutionary movement to offer them? Its basic unit was the *kruzhok*, the small circle of devotees who would meet, discuss, carry on impassioned arguments on philosophy or politics late into the night. Hermetic and secretive because of the oppressive political atmosphere of tsarist Russia, these circles were warm and supportive internally, yet also (with equal and opposite animus) chronically suspicious of outsiders, especially of neighbouring circles with rival programmes.

When they originated in the 1840s, the *kruzhki* derived their ideas from German idealist philosophy, which they embraced with a fervour no doubt intensified by the abject condition of the Russian Orthodox Church. It is almost as if there were a church-shaped vacuum in nineteenth-century Russian society. In effect the radicals channelled their religious aspirations into a philosophy of secular utopianism, promising social revolution as the means of man's final deliverance from evil.

Official censorship ensured that no such ideal could be openly put forward. The nearest radical thinkers could come to the public avowal of their aspirations was in literature – or, to be more accurate, through the literary journals, which were actually by no means purely literary, but combined prose, poetry and drama with social, philosophical and scientific treatises and with informed comment on the issues of the day. Literature absorbed some of the religious impulses which the Church was unable to channel: as a recent student of Tolstoy has commented, 'much of the finest fiction of the period was in essence theology in narrative form'.[19] And Vissarion Belinskii, one of the founders of the radical movement, went so far as to claim that 'all our moral interests, our whole spiritual life, have been focused exclusively on literature, and it will probably long remain so: literature is the living fount from which all human feelings and concepts flow into society'.[20]

If with literature the intelligentsia entered a marriage of convenience which developed into a passion, it was also extremely attracted by the prospects of science, especially after Russia's defeat in the Crimean War discredited the autocracy and opened the way for the tsarist version of perestroika in the great reforms of Alexander II, which did much to renew the Petrine vision of the state as the engineer of social progress. Radicals were drawn by both the natural and social sciences: the first for its promise of industrial development and increased mastery over nature, the second for the assurance it purported to offer of progress towards a more humane society. 'Without science,' the early Russian socialist Alexander Herzen once said, 'there is no salvation for modern man.'[21]

Their earnest zeal was not unlike that of the English Utilitarians: they wanted to jettison tradition and superstition in favour of hard-headed, realistic work to better the people on scientific principles. With no parliament to implement reform, however, most of them believed this goal could only be achieved by overthrowing the autocracy. Hence the need for revolution.

The man who best united in his person all these aspirations was Nikolai Chernyshevskii. He was the son of a clergyman, a seminarist who abandoned the priestly calling because he lost his faith both in God and in the Church. Like Marx, he regarded political economy as an extension of the natural sciences, a source of certain knowledge and soundly attested principles for ensuring social progress. Himself an editor of *Sovremennik* (*The Contemporary*), the leading radical journal of its day, he also published a novel, *Chto Delat'?* (*What is to be Done?*), which captured the imagination of two generations of radical youth. In it he shows how young women, emancipated from the oppressive patriarchal rule of their fathers, pool their resources, work together and share their income in a seamstresses' co-operative, or *artel'*. This co-operative Chernyshevskii presents as a model primary cell, a pre-figuration of the human future society whose advent is being prepared by the austere young intellectuals, in fact revolutionaries, whom he calls euphemistically 'the new people'.

It is here that the foundations were laid for the secular utopian project of the Communists. Lenin greatly valued *Chto Delat'?*. 'This novel provides inspiration for a lifetime,' he once remarked.[22] He called his doctrine 'scientific socialism' and insisted that 'Marxism is all-powerful because it is *true*'. And Bukharin and Preobrazhenskii, authors of the first popular guide to Soviet Communism, roundly asserted that Communism, being scientific, had finally replaced religion: 'Scientific Communism . . . is guided by the data of the natural sciences, which are in irreconcilable conflict with all religious imaginings.'[23]

The regime which Lenin founded generated a singularly frustrating milieu for the intelligentsia. In one sense, they were the creators of the system, the custodians of its ideals, and many of them tried to live up to that calling. Yet at the same time, they were collectivised and oppressed, just like the peasants, their own ideals turned against them and used for their enserfment. Some of them – often the compliant and untalented – were co-opted by the regime in order to organise and supervise the rest. Under Stalin, they were required to peddle a crude, paranoid and reductionist view of the world, in which the utopian vision of the Old Bolsheviks was converted into a propaganda instrument to justify the regime's authority.

One of the most important and damaging aspects of this manipulated utopianism was its relentless drive into the future, given administrative form in the series of Five Year Plans begun in 1928. The science of economics played very little part in the elaboration of these Plans: they were not based on a projection of present productive trends into the future, nor did they attempt to balance one sector with another (industry, say, with housing or food supply). Rather the first Five Year Plan (in particular) represented what the economist Naum Jasny has called 'Bacchanalian planning': setting apparently impossible targets in certain key heavy industrial sectors, and letting everything else line up behind.[24] 'There are no fortresses which Bolsheviks cannot storm,' Stalin exhorted.

This obsession with heavy industry and with the future was achieved at the cost of crushing everything which conflicted with it: the peasant community, serious intellectual life, the natural environment, even in a sense history itself. The advance into the future acquired a sacral character, measured out in five year spans. Both past and present were important only for what they contributed to the Great Future.

The state monopoly of information and mass communications, backed by a vigilant security police, made any serious intellectual or cultural life impossible. The conflict of diverse viewpoints and the assimilation of uncomfortable facts, both prerequisites for the formation of public opinion and the conduct of serious politics, were altogether precluded. While some intellectuals were fanatically devoted to the cause, others merely professed opinions, no longer quite knowing what they really thought, and succumbed to apathy and cynicism, or to the ambivalence which George Orwell so aptly termed 'doublethink'.

The Stalinist degradation of intellectual life wrought terrible destruction in the intelligentsia's own sanctuaries of science and literature. In science the nadir was reached with Lysenkoism, a pseudo-biology based on the theory, unproven by experiment, that man himself can intervene and direct the process of genetic change – a notion fully consonant with Stalin's slogan about fortresses and Bolsheviks.[25]

In literature, the authoritatively imposed doctrine of 'socialist realism' made obligatory a banal and sugary mode of writing, while the Writers' Union made the text a kind of collective product, on which writer, editor, censor, reviewer, party cell and literary critic all left their mark.[26]

Yet in the long run, science and literature were to prove to be channels by which intellectual emancipation re-entered Soviet society. In a way, it was natural that this should be so. Science and literature cannot serve even the purposes for which the regime requires them while they are confined in the totalitarian straitjacket. A science which is not up to international standards, which is not meticulously verified by experiment and not open to new information and argument, cannot nourish a productive economy nor (even more important) sustain strong armed forces. In literature, which is by nature semantically rich and often ambiguous, the authoritative imposition of the banal and monological text becomes self-defeating. It no longer fulfils even its intended pedagogical function because it undermines normal communication between writer and reader. Readers no longer look for information in what the text states, but rather in what it implies or even omits. They become insensitive to the deadeningly omnipresent norm, reacting only to the fleeting aberration.[27]

In one respect the Stalin period brought a disguised blessing to the intelligentsia. In the nineteenth century they had tended to idealise the *narod*, the common people, aspiring to serve or emancipate them, while not really *knowing* them. In Soviet society, and particularly under Stalin, they could not avoid close acquaintance with the *narod*, being forced into unsought intimacy with them in schools, army, building sites and labour camps.

I have dwelt at length on the traditions of the peasantry and the intelligentsia because they underlie such habits of community as have survived at all into the modern Soviet Union. These traditions played a decisive role in making the Russian revolution and in shaping Soviet society. Even under Stalin, though distorted and abused, they did not die out altogether. When one seeks to understand the present Soviet crisis, one must take them into account once again, for a new society can only be constructed out of the materials which are to hand. Furthermore, the reconquest of memory has to begin there too.

3

The return
of the repressed

In Stalin's time, any real sense of community among the intelligentsia was rendered virtually impossible by the massive mistrust which the ubiquitous security police informers aroused. Since people could not be sure who might be reporting on them, they tended to keep social contacts down to a minimum. Ordinary human solidarity was confined either to specially trusted close friends or to Fainsod's 'mutual protection associations': informal coteries of officials helping each other out by covering up each other's mistakes and shortcomings. Stalin, of course, tried to break such islands of passive resistance to his rule: that was one of the aims of his purges. But no regime, no matter how tyrannical, can succeed in eliminating all such improvisations.

However, after Stalin's death, with the mitigation of terror, something more like normal social life gradually resumed. Among the intelligentsia, rapidly growing at this time with the expansion of higher education, it usually took the form of evening gatherings of colleagues or friends round a table loaded with black bread, sausage meat, cucumber, whatever happened to be available in the sparsely stocked grocery shops. They would discuss everything under the sun – literature, philosophy, science, religion – but especially the latest political events and all the frustrations of everyday life. These penurious salons had little to offer gastronomically, but they were, in the words of a participant, 'sumptuous, endless feasts of the spirit. In these circles theories were propounded and disputed, old authorities were felled and new ones erected.'[1]

This was classical soil for the matchless Soviet anecdotes, in which the oppressed cocked a snook at their oppressors and mocked the infuriating anomalies of Soviet life. Let just one, which I heard many times, illustrate the boundless paranoia of the authorities and the helplessness of the victims under Stalin. Three men are sitting in a prison cell and talking about their past. 'Why were you arrested?' 'Because I was late for work, so they accused me of sabotage. And you?' 'Oh, I arrived early for work, so they accused me of being a spy.' They both turn to the third cell-mate: 'And what happened to you?' 'I arrived for work punctually, but in their eyes my zeal was just a cloak to conceal my hostility to Communism.'

This was the time of Khrushchev's so-called 'secret speech' – actually not very secret though not published till 1989. People sought each other out and tried to understand what had happened to them all in the whirlwind years of war, purges and officially sponsored falsehood. Their exchanges of thought and experience were soon seasoned by the accounts of those returning piecemeal from labour camps, able to tell of a nether circle of the Stalinist inferno which everyone had dimly guessed at, but which few had survived to bear witness to. Among those homespun chroniclers of the underworld were even a few singers, bards with guitars, who refashioned popular ditties through the medium of the labour camp song, and thus resurrected long-submerged folk wisdom in modern guise: a Soviet version of the blues, if you like.[2]

It was also the time when more and more Soviet citizens were acquiring short-wave radio sets and listening to foreign broadcasts. More was becoming known about the present and recent past, enough to stimulate animated gossip without fully satisfying anyone's curiosity. The business of exchanging information thus assumed a crucial import-ance. The assimilation and mutual discussion of uncomfortable truths – a prerequisite for the formation of public opinion anywhere – was resumed for the first time since the twenties. This was the essence of the apparently aimless conversations which Russians call *tryop*. The ignor-ance and 'opinionlessness' of isolation was being overcome. As the human rights activist Lyudmila Alekseeva puts it: 'These conversations helped one to grope towards an understanding of the nature of Soviet society, how one should live in it, what one could accept and what reject.'[3]

In this setting *samizdat* developed almost spontaneously. Indeed, one could regard it as a natural extension of conversation, born of the desire to fix little-known information, put new ideas into circulation (even if very limited), remember and disseminate unpublished literature, whether of the past or of the present. The technology was primitive: one person would type four or five copies, each more faded than the last, and pass them on to friends, who, if they felt strongly enough about the material, would repeat the process. Whole journals and even novels were circulated in this way. So inadequate was the supply that one might be offered a 300-page novel for just one night to read: then one would invite the friends one trusted and sit up, passing pages from one to another. An ideal milieu for the formation of tightly knit circles – *kruzhki* – with their own ardently held views. Again, the setting was very reminiscent of that which had given birth to the nineteenth-century radicals, though the terrible lessons of the Stalin years were to lead their successors to very different political conclusions.

Such gatherings existed not only in Moscow and Leningrad, but also in a few Russian provincial towns, in Ukraine, in the cities of the Baltic and the Transcaucasus, where they helped to generate a much sharper awareness of national culture, history and tradition. The first cells of a potential civic society were germinating, but because of the totalitarian soil in which they were embedded, they were still isolated and helpless, often ignorant even of each other's existence.

The post-Khrushchev leadership took the decision to criminalise these activities – or at least their outgrowth, the dissemination of *samizdat* – without, however, restoring indiscriminate mass terror. This decision converted the more determined and self-aware of the participants in these gatherings into what became known as 'dissidents'. The turning point was a cultural one: the arrest in 1965 of two writers, Andrei Sinyavskii and Yulii Daniel', for allowing their *samizdat* not only to circulate among friends, but to be published in the west under pseudonyms. The event soon became widely known, thanks to western radio stations. Professional people, and writers in particular, were afraid that it might herald a return to Stalinist methods of secret trials, savage sentences and the victimisation of friends and relatives. They wanted to try to ensure that the proceedings would be public and that the court would at least observe the laws under which it claimed to operate.

This was an important new development. The idea that the Soviet authorities should observe their own laws was a novel one, and it struck them at a vulnerable point. Anxious to prevent for good and all the resumption of illegalities on a Stalinist scale, Khrushchev had launched a programme of 'socialist legality', which his successors endorsed. So to be publicly seen to be overriding the law in Stalinist style was something they wished to avoid. But this enabled individuals for the first time to behave as if the Soviet constitution were a serious document, as if they were citizens of a free country. Such behaviour, as the human rights activist Vladimir Bukovskii later commented, 'presupposed a small core of freedom in each individual'.[4]

The authorities' relative restraint and the protesters' boldness made possible the first political demonstration in the Soviet Union since the twenties. It took place on 5 December 1965 at the Pushkin monument in Moscow, with banners demanding 'Glasnost for the trial of Sinyavskii and Daniel'!' and 'Respect the Soviet constitution!' There was scarcely time to read them, though, before the banners were torn down and the demonstrators were bundled off to police vans.

At the trial itself the new human rights activists were not admitted, and they had to stamp their feet in the freezing cold outside the court room, where, however, they timidly made their first acquaintance with western correspondents, a significant expansion of their channels of communication.[5] Despite the difficulties, Alexander Ginsburg, who had already been imprisoned under Khrushchev for issuing a *samizdat* journal, succeeded in making a transcript of the trial, revealing its judicial irregularities, and compiling the letters and press comment it provoked at home and abroad. In this way he breached the regime's monopoly of information, filling in what George Orwell would have called a 'memory hole' (but what in current Soviet parlance is referred to as a 'blank spot') before it was created. He distributed his so-called White Book among friends, sent copies to the Soviet leaders, and made sure that some reached the west, where it was published for re-smuggling into the Soviet Union.

Altogether, then, the Sinyavskii–Daniel' trial brought concerned individuals together, gave them the watchwords of 'publicity' and 'legality', and opened up the possibility of continued communication with each other, with the outside world, and even indirectly with Soviet society itself. Sympathy for the accused became a moral basis for the formation of *kruzhki*. As one witness has commented, 'it was the ethical gauge by which young intellectuals chose one another's association. To denounce the trial privately was to give oneself an identity badge that like-minded people could recognise.'[6]

Therewith the pattern was set for the gradual emergence of an alternative public opinion, a crucially important process for understanding what is taking place now. Its centre of gravity was initially human rights, but this concept expanded in due course to embrace issues of nationality, religion, culture, the environment – issues which people gradually articulated more clearly to themselves and to each other as they acquired ever more diverse information, exchanged opinions, and gained a sense of mutual solidarity.

Adopting such viewpoints meant, of course, in the long run that the human rights movement could not remain unified. In view of the size and diversity of the Soviet Union, this was inevitable. But in the short term immediate needs united the various participants. The focus of the movement throughout was the *samizdat* journal austerely called *The Chronicle of Current Events*, which first appeared in 1968. It bore on its masthead Article 19 of the UN Declaration on Human Rights: 'Everyone has the right to freedom of opinion and expression; this right includes freedom to hold opinions without interference and to seek, receive and impart information and ideas through any medium regardless of frontiers.' Otherwise eschewing any explicit editorial policy, this crudely produced typewritten bulletin collated and presented without comment examples of the Soviet authorities violating their own laws in their dealings with citizens. Natalya Gorbanevskaya, the first editor, would turn out seven copies on her typewriter, one for herself, one for a western correspondent, and five for friends, who were expected to retype their copies in similar fashion and pass them on. The journal's distribution channels functioned in the reverse direction as channels of information. To judge by the growing number of locations which furnished information for its pages, its circulation became more widespread over the years. According to one estimate, it may have attained as many as 10,000 copies by the early eighties, with perhaps ten readers for each copy.[7]

Lyudmila Alekseeva, one of its editors, has testified that working for the *Chronicle* 'meant to pledge oneself to be faithful to the truth, to cleanse oneself of the filth of doublethink which has pervaded every aspect of Soviet life . . . This created among people who scarcely knew one another, but who were connected with the *Chronicle*, very strong spiritual ties of the kind that probably existed among the early Christians.'[8]

With this loose co-ordinating centre in place, the movement was able in the seventies to diversify into specialised groups, some dealing with national rights, others with women's rights, invalids' rights, the rights of religious believers and of those confined in mental hospitals. Many of these produced their own specialist journals on the general pattern of the *Chronicle*. The Soviet government's signing of a European Security Agreement at Helsinki in 1975, with clauses on human rights and the free contact of peoples, provided an international validation for their concerns, and imparted renewed impetus to their work. A number of Helsinki Monitoring Groups appeared in various Soviet republics.

The Soviet authorities were embarrassed by the movement, and had difficulty in dealing with it effectively. The KGB was like a huge regular army faced with guerrillas, unable to place consistent informers in the network, and too centralised and clumsy to trace the informal, decentralised and unauthoritarian pattern of its contacts. Besides, to try to break it by mass arrests would have risked returning to Stalinist terror.

They reacted therefore with apparently piecemeal and haphazard sanctions: arrests here, expulsions from the party there, job dismissals elsewhere, in some cases psychiatric confinement or enforced exile from the Soviet Union.

This pressure did not succeed in breaking the dissenting movement, indeed if anything the reverse is true, but it did begin to change its nature during the late seventies and early eighties. Participants began to go underground, seeking anonymity as a natural response to the increasing inevitability of sanctions against them. The movement's social composition began to change as ordinary workers and employees began to become involved. And it moved away from a primary concern with human rights towards an involvement in socio-economic, environmental and practical problems.

In 1977 the Donbass coal-mining engineer Vladimir Klebanov established the first independent trade union. It began, in traditional dissenting style, by protesting openly about violations of the legal rights of employees: it was formed by workers whose pursuit of justice against their employers had brought them to the waiting-room of the Presidium of the Supreme Soviet in Moscow. Most of its members were detained on various pretexts soon after the foundation of the Union, and Klebanov himself was confined in a mental hospital.[9]

In the light of that experience, the second attempt to set up a free trade union took a different course. The Free Inter-Professional Association of Workers (known as SMOT) soon ceased to publish the names of its members, and confined itself to offering legal advice and to publishing surveys of socio-economic problems – for example, on food supply difficulties, price rises and rationing.[10] SMOT has survived to the present day, and thus provides a link between the dissenting movement and the rise of the 'informal associations'.

The human rights movement drew its strength from the cultural and scientific intelligentsia. Of its initial activists, the signatories of protest letters in the late sixties, more than half were scholars, many of them natural scientists, and a quarter were writers.[11] The public tribune of the movement was Andrei Sakharov, whose nuclear weapons work had alerted him to the unscrupulous and irresponsible way in which the Soviet leaders were exploiting the formidable technological power at their disposal. He had become convinced that only resolute defence of human rights could render governments accountable to their peoples, and thus restrain them from mortally dangerous abuses of power. The sight of his bald head outside a courtroom was a source of comfort to a good many dissenters.

Few scientists had Sakharov's saintly single-mindedness, but as a social stratum they were unusually well placed to identify abuses of power, and they enjoyed the prestige, the confidence of being indispensable, which enabled them to voice their concern. In the late sixties, scientific institutes became for a time centres of human rights protest activity. The authorities would react, sometimes with job dismissals and expulsions from the party, but more often with milder penalties, such as official rebukes, which at least left those affected still holding their jobs and able to pursue further research. There is some evidence that quiet resistance by academic councils and even by party organisations within the Academy itself dissuaded the authorities from taking harsher reprisals.[12]

Most striking is the fact that the Academy of Sciences, though it did not treat Sakharov well, never expelled him from membership, even at the time of his deepest official disgrace. This was not necessarily a sign of civic courage: more likely it was a defence of privilege. But still, the life tenure of academicians is a rallying cry which, however unheroic, in practice limits the power of the party and establishes a tiny bridgehead for political pluralism.

Of course, the great majority of scientists were not involved directly in human rights agitation and did not become open dissenters. But once Stalin's mass terror had ended, many of them shut themselves away in their institutes to devote themselves, along with a few like-minded colleagues, to what they considered promising fields of research, regardless of ideological implications. Whole branches of science, neglected or suppressed under Stalin – cybernetics, genetics, the social sciences – were revived and discreetly cultivated. In some of these new fields, even or perhaps especially ones which accorded ill with Marxist ideology, Soviet science established itself as a world leader, as in literary theory and semiotics, thanks to the seminar of Professor Yurii Lotman at Tartu University in Estonia.[13]

Another more practical example was the work of the Institute of Economics and Industrial Organisation at the Academy of Sciences in Novosibirsk. After Avel' Aganbegyan was appointed its director in 1967, it became the leading centre for research into what might be called the 'socialist market economy', as distinct from the centrally administered model which Stalin had introduced and Brezhnev was restoring. Every month the institute produced a journal which gained a world-wide reputation for its penetrating analyses of Soviet economic weaknesses and its propounding of alternatives. In 1983 the institute sent a long report to the post-Brezhnev leaders, written by Tatyana Zaslavskaya, Aganbegyan's colleague, devastatingly critical of the state of the economy, and recommending radical decentralisation. In many ways this report laid the foundation stone for the current economic reforms. Non-conformist work, long discreetly pursued, thus fed into the mainstream of perestroika.[14]

If scientists were able to get away comparatively lightly with such free-thinking enquiry, it was because the work they were doing was important to the political leaders, and also because scientists quite simply enjoyed a high standing which pre-dated the origins of the Communist Party. Much the same kind of prestige attaches to writers, which explains why the institutions of literature, and especially the 'thick journals', became the other major centres of what might be called 'establishment non-conformity'.

The Soviet 'thick journal' has a certain Victorian quality to it. It would look far more familiar to subscribers of the *Quarterly Review* than to today's periodical readers in Britain. It is a kind of monthly intellectual hamper of goodies which lands on the doormat. Predominantly but by no means purely literary, it combines prose, poetry and drama with criticism, reviews and comment on the great issues of the day. Social, philosophical and scientific problems are grist to its mill. If controversial, they are often tackled in the form of literary criticism, which is a convenient and acceptable camouflage.

This has made the 'thick journal' the ideal forum for discussing the more serious problems of Soviet society. Until very recently such discussions had to be couched in an oblique and allusory style, to circumvent the censorship, and this has made them difficult for outsiders to follow. In a sense, though, their enigmatic quality was part of the mystique which journals found it expedient to cultivate, involving readers in an intellectual cryptogram accessible to a quite numerous but still limited circle of initiates and fellow believers. So each journal evolved not only its own political attitude, but also its own distinctive clientele, its relationship with whom created a kind of social magnetic field.

The most celebrated example of the type was *Novyi mir* (*New World*), especially in the sixties under the editorship of Alexander Tvardovskii. Tvardovskii was the son of a peasant expropriated during the collectivisation of agriculture and deported to Siberia, so that he experienced personally the harsh realities of the Stalin era. This did not prevent him being a loyal Communist, and a very popular war poet, whose literary hero, the peasant lad Vasilii Tyorkin, a kind of Tommy Atkins of the Red Army, was to be found in the knapsack of many a Soviet soldier. Tvardovskii's party loyalty was, however, of a distinctive variety. He interpreted party-mindedness in literature to mean telling the truth about what the ordinary people had undergone in the upheavals of Soviet history, not concealing the suffering Stalin had inflicted on them. Such frankness was officially tolerated as long as Khrushchev's de-Stalinisation was in progress, but Tvardovskii persisted with it, even deepened it, after Khrushchev's fall in 1964.

I was a Moscow University student myself at that time, and I recall with what eagerness the monthly arrival of the pale blue volume was awaited. One had to be a personal subscriber: there was no chance of buying a spare copy at a bookstall. On the evidence of readers' letters, Vladimir Lakshin, Tvardovskii's deputy, has asserted that *Novyi mir* 'became part of people's lives' and 'inspired a faith in the indestructibility of the truth'. I too remember the earnest enthusiasm of its loyal readers. In a world where everyone knew the public media were full of distortions and evasions, Tvardovskii's skill and courage in fighting for authors in whom he believed kept open a unique channel of unclogged communication. 'Novyi mir was read in the corridors of power, in remote villages, and in the most distant provinces, and its readership spanned labourers on construction sites, librarians, village schoolteachers, agronomists, passionate lovers of truth and lonely seekers after faith.'[15]

Perhaps his greatest contribution to Soviet culture was to make possible a serious re-examination of the Stalin period. Alexander Solzhenitsyn's story A Day in the Life of Ivan Denisovich, which Tvardovskii personally steered through formidable political obstacles, recounted candidly the routine of a Stalinist labour camp in all its squalor and inhumanity. The publication in 1962 of this sober but cogent aperçu released a flood of popular memory. Thousands of ordinary Soviet citizens wrote heartfelt letters to Solzhenitsyn, thanking him in glowing terms for daring to disclose what they had lived through but had never ventured to talk of openly. Many of them appended their own detailed accounts, providing for Solzhenitsyn the first of the materials he later wove into his much more comprehensive survey, The Gulag Archipelago.

Overnight Solzhenitsyn became, as it were, honorary archivist for a nation which had lacked its own memory. This was the 'return of the repressed', not in the individual psyche, but in the cultural community. And as Freud has taught us, the repressed always returns with tremendous emotional force. Such was certainly the reaction of Solzhenitsyn's readers to Ivan Denisovich:

'I could not sit still. I kept leaping up, walking about and imagining all those scenes as taking place in the camp I myself was in.'

'Now I read and weep, but when I was imprisoned in Ukhta, for ten years I shed not a tear.'

'After reading it, the only thing left to do is to knock a nail into the wall, tie a knot and hang oneself.'

'Although I wept when I read it, I felt myself a citizen with full rights among other people.'[16]

Tvardovskii and *Novyi mir* performed another signal service for the folk memory, and that was the cultivation of a school of rural authors, peasants by origin, who had risen with the precipitate upward social mobility of the Soviet era to receive their training at the Gor'kii Institute of Literature and to become writers. Their personal experience bridged a profound chasm in Soviet society, between the urban and the rural. For millions of Soviet citizens alive today, the decisive life event was the migration from village to town, usually at an early age, initially to do military service or to acquire an education, after completing which they would not return home, but would move heaven and earth to find a job in town and somewhere to live – often enduring years, even a lifetime, in crowded and sub-standard accommodation in order to realise their ambition. In a sense, their feat of individual dedication to the urban ideal replicated the total historical experience of Soviet society, with its worship of industry, technology, education and culture. Both in the macrocosm and the microcosm, this dedication was achieved at the cost not only of turning one's back on rural life, but also of denigrating it, devaluing it as something from which to escape at all costs. How many Soviet citizens have, in this way, denied their own childhood?

The village writers thus tapped a deep and long blocked up stream of feeling. Their leisurely evocations of the work and customs of the peasant community stimulated a strong reaction among readers who had once known that way of life, or had heard their parents talk about it. Again, this was a kind of 'return of the repressed', for the values of the village community had been repressed for at least a generation, partly because the official ideology imposed such amnesia, but partly also because individuals making their way in the modern world preferred to turn their backs resolutely on what they were abandoning.

The intensity of the reception given to 'village prose' also owed a good deal to the perception that the urban world had not brought with it the unclouded contentment of the utopian vision. Far from it: by the mid-sixties, when the Soviet Union was at last becoming a predominantly urban society, towns seemed to entail ugliness, pollution, stress, loneliness, alcoholism, delinquency and unstable family life. Such at least was a widespread impression. Many Soviet writers of the last generation have been actuated by motives similar to those of our own Victorian novelists: by fear of a new kind of contagious moral and spiritual disorder, spread by the teeming industrial towns. They strove to combat this disease by reasserting values inherited from an earlier, ostensibly more stable and humane era. Among these values was traditional religious belief: a vague, non-denominational but unmistakable Christianity. At a stroke the Promethean Soviet drive towards the future had been inverted, had become the worship of a lost Golden Age!

Altogether, the Brezhnev years may have been an era of stagnation, but they were also one of convalescence. A society which had been atomised and traumatised under Stalin was slowly and painfully reconstituting its memory and reknitting the fabric of social solidarity. It turned out that the Soviet people were not afflicted by total amnesia. A dim sense of loss of community was reawakening, together with an intellectual inheritance which had not completely succumbed to the totalitarian rewriting of history. So a certain basis did exist for the revival of autonomous social institutions and eventually of genuine politics. The preoccupation with human rights was the first sign of recovery, but it gradually broadened to embrace underlying issues of nationality, religion, culture and the natural environment. The articulation of these concerns will form the subject matter of the next three chapters.

4

A civil society
in embryo

In 1987 a great turning point was reached in Soviet history. The government passed a decree banning tree felling around Lake Baikal and requiring the Baikal Pulp and Paper Combine to phase out the production of cellulose.[1] Hardly the stuff of historic turning points, you might think. It doesn't sound all that sensational, I must admit. But if you consider the implications for a moment, it actually contradicts the relentless drive towards economic growth which Soviet Communists have always regarded as a paramount priority. Lenin after all was fond of saying that 'Communism equals Soviet power plus electrification of the whole country'. And that meant accepting everything which electrification and the accompanying forms of modernisation entailed.

Nor is Baikal the only example of this kind. As I shall explain below, the great project to divert the north-flowing rivers southward to irrigate the semi-arid areas of Central Asia and the Volga basin has been halted, if not finally cancelled. And the nuclear power programme, crucial to the Soviet Union's energy needs, has faltered since the explosion in the Chernobyl' power station. In fact, some of the most cherished ambitions of the Soviet regime are being seriously challenged. How did this come about?

In the formative years of the Soviet system, and especially during the thirties and forties, the primacy of economic growth was so undisputed that no heed whatever was paid to environmental damage resulting from industrial development. The predominant attitude to nature was that it was there to be conquered! Nor in any case were the cumulative effects of pollution readily apparent at first. Blast furnaces, power stations and chemical plants were built at frenzied speed and left to belch their fumes into the air and discharge their effluents into the rivers. Lenin's 'electrification of the whole country' was pursued at headlong pace. Films were made and poems were composed about Dneproges, the hydroelectric project on the lower River Dnieper which was one of the great showpieces of the first Five Year Plan, but no one at the time deemed it worth mentioning that thousands of acres of agricultural land and forest had been destroyed to make way for it. Equivalent degradation could result from poorly executed irrigation and drainage schemes. In Central Asia the intensive irrigation of cotton plantations has gradually deprived Lake Aral of its normal water inflow, so that much of the lake has become brackish marsh or even desert. And the marshy Polesye area of Belorussia has been so ineptly drained that in places sand dunes have formed and even dust storms have developed. As a local wit commented, aping the propaganda machine: 'In the next Five Year Plan let us transform all the marshes of Belorussia into deserts!'[2]

In the early sixties, though, a few writers and scientists began to sound a warning note. One reason for this was mounting disillusionment inside the party with Khrushchev's headstrong character, his refusal to heed the advice of scientists about the damaging side effects of his grandiose projects. Take, for example, his much trumpeted programme for sowing vast areas of western Siberia with grain – the so-called virgin lands – which caused massive soil erosion because elementary precautions were not taken. But this was not just Khrushchev's personal foible. In his own idiosyncratic way he was only reflecting a general characteristic of the system: the fascination with size and speed, the drive to construct everything as big as possible and as fast as possible. This drive was institutionalised, it was inherent in the political structure: any ministry which was made responsible for a major project would automatically receive increased funding and additional personnel. Ministerial empire-building had its own logic, regardless of the effects any particular scheme might have on the rest of the economy or on the environment, and regardless even of whether it had any prospect of ultimately paying for itself. This is a classic example of the complete absence of checks and balances within the totalitarian system: although laws existed to protect nature, any powerful minister who could persuade the party's ruling bodies of the desirability of his pet project would receive an unconditional green light for its implementation.

The object of the first ever environmental campaign in the Soviet Union was the very same Lake Baikal which the government finally agreed in 1987 to protect. The purity of Baikal's water was threatened by careless timber felling and by the effluent from two planned cellulose factories designed to produce especially tough cord for the tyres of heavy bombers. Interestingly enough, it was conservative and Russian nationalist writers who first raised the alarm: the Siberian V. Chivilikhin[3] and Mikhail Sholokhov, who made an impassioned appeal at the 23rd Party Congress in 1966: 'Our descendants will not forgive us if we do not preserve this glorious lake, this sacred Baikal.' A number of the Soviet Union's best known scientists, such as Academicians Berg, Zel'dovich and Kapitsa, issued statements in support of them. A scientists' committee was set up to defend the lake, and Andrei Sakharov went personally to make representations to Brezhnev.[4]

This has been a quarter-century-long battle royal: on the one side are ranged the strategic imperatives of the military-industrial complex, with its grip on the party apparatus, on the other the status of Baikal as the world's largest reservoir of fresh water, home to unique forms of aquatic life, and backed by well-informed writers and scientists. By the time the censorship was tightened again during the late sixties, Baikal had already become a *cause célèbre* and could not just be stuffed back into the bottle. It was the first occasion in Soviet history on which it was recognised, at least by some participants in the controversy, that national pride and maximum industrial production might be in conflict with one another.

The result has been a prolonged and somewhat muffled war of attrition between the industrial ministries and the ecological campaigners. Today the campaigners are headed by the Siberian novelist Valentin Rasputin, who complains that, as a result, he has very little time left for his creative writing. It has been a long story of official decisions to reduce pollution of Baikal being stealthily circumnavigated by industrial ministries eager to maximise their output and minimise their expenditure, and until recently able to count on uninquisitive public media.[5] In 1987 the campaigners achieved a success in the form of the government decree which I described as a turning point. But even this is not total victory. Rasputin himself reports that the new combination of supervision from above, *and from below by the public*, is at last producing results, but he also warns that the battle to ensure beneficial decisions are actually implemented is far from over. 'Baikal is like a battlefield where a ceasefire has just been declared. Some are observing it, but others have got used to sniping and find it inconvenient to change their way of life.'[6]

Over the years environmentalists have been able to establish a foothold partly because their concerns reflect genuine economic dilemmas of the kind that pitch one ministry against another and therefore divide the party leadership. The American political scientist Thane Gustafson has pointed out that what appear to be pressure groups in the Soviet Union cannot actually become effective unless the party leadership is genuinely uncertain or divided about which of two alternative policies to adopt. As he rightly remarks, 'this is not pressure group politics, but the politics of waiting for the open window'.[7]

Apart from Baikal, one or two other 'open windows' have appeared during the last twenty years or so, and a semi-tolerated public debate has been taking place. During the sixties, for instance, it became possible to cast doubt on the advisability of constructing huge hydroelectric power stations. The institution responsible for them, Gidroproekt, had originally been part of the immense NKVD economic network, which included Stalin's labour camps, and it inherited from those days an imperious and secretive manner.[8] Criticism of Gidroproekt became possible mainly because other equally powerful agencies found their own interests impaired by its activities. The Ministry of Fisheries discovered that its catches were declining in the lower reaches of rivers dammed upstream. The timber industry lost valuable sources of raw material. And the higher priority which Khrushchev assigned to agriculture alerted everyone to the loss of fertile arable land.

It still needed a scholar of insight and pertinacity to crystallise this opposition. This was Academician Vendrov, of the Institute of Water Problems, who made it his business to assemble information and direct it to influential quarters, as well as training graduate students to support and continue his work. According to Gustafson, who interviewed some of them: 'In the early seventies Vendrov's students were filled with a crusading spirit. They saw themselves as the front line defence of the environment, and had detailed knowledge of the work done by similar groups in the west.' Being a member of an advisory panel attached to the State Planning Committee (Gosplan) Vendrov was able to press his points home at the highest level, and to contribute, perhaps decisively, to a moderation of the all-powerful hydroelectric urge.[9]

One environmental battle which has especially fired the public imagination was fought over the proposed diversion of Russia's northern rivers. It has been one of Russia's great geographic misfortunes that most of its major rivers flow unproductively into the Arctic Ocean, while large areas of the Volga basin and Central Asia are semi-arid or worse. Even in tsarist times one or two engineers had put forward schemes for diverting some of these rivers so that part of their flow went southwards; and a Communist regime which prided itself on its ability to 'transform nature' was not likely to remain permanently resigned to the cussedness of geography.

The only problem from the government's point of view was the breathtaking cost of the hydraulic works required. However, the 25th Party Congress in 1976 felt affluent enough to order full-scale scientific studies of the possibility of diverting water from the rivers Ob', Irtysh, and perhaps Enisei, through a 2000-kilometre-long canal to flow into the Aral and Caspian Seas, with feeders to provide irrigation for the cotton-growing areas of Central Asia and for the industrial towns of Western Siberia. An auxiliary project was also envisaged, to divert northern European Russian rivers towards the Volga basin.[10]

Among the project's principal protagonists were the Central Asian

Communist Party organisations, eager to receive cheap supplies of water to sustain a wasteful and corrupt local economy resting on the over-planting of cotton. But most influential of all was Minvodkhoz, the Ministry of Water Resources and Melioration. This ministry is one of the prime Soviet leviathans. Responsible for all hydraulic, irrigation and drainage work throughout the country, it employs by its own account one and a half million people, including building workers, which I estimate at something approaching one per cent of the entire Soviet population of working age. When I spoke to some of its leading officials in May 1988, they were unbowed by recent setbacks and confident that the country would one day recognise again the need for river diversions and come running back to them for help. They were polite but unmistakably scornful about the temporary fashion for taking notice of ignorant amateurs expressing opinions on such complex matters. No doubt that would pass, they implied. Meanwhile, they were stockpiling the feasibility reports of no less than 150 research institutes on various aspects of the project, against the day when they would be needed. Even casting an eye over these mounds of paper, I could sense the sheer scope of the patronage that lies stored up in a project like this, capable of employing and paying hundreds of thousands of people for many years.

Initially the opponents of Minvodkhoz took longer to make their views felt. Economists have always tended to oppose the project, reckoning there must be cheaper ways of preserving water, and over the years they have signalled their reservations in specialist journals. But once again, it was natural scientists and writers who were eventually more successful in making opposition effective. The writer Vasilii Belov – ecological spokesman for northern Russia as Rasputin is for Siberia – was especially worried about the monasteries and churches of his homeland, most of which lie along river banks and hence are vulnerable to any rise in the water level. Unable to publish his views in the Soviet press, he eventually resorted in the summer of 1982 to an émigré newspaper in Paris.[11] Under Gorbachev such subterfuges became unnecessary, and the Writers' Union congress of summer 1986 turned into a concerted forum for public opposition to river diversions.

'Glasnost is all very well,' complained Rasputin, 'but what use is it if nothing changes as a result?'[12]

Scientists were also stirring themselves to take advantage of the new political conjuncture. They were worried about the effects of flooding on the soil, and about the dangers to the world climate of curtailing the flow of so much relatively warm water into the Arctic Ocean. The Academy of Sciences held interdisciplinary seminars in 1985, which aroused such interest and concern that a voluntary commission was set up under Academician Yanshin to study the whole project and present an alternative report on it. This commission brought together specialists from a variety of fields: soil science, geography, biology, ethnography, law and so on. One of its members, to whom I talked, emphasised that it was a voluntary enterprise, set up from below out of shared concern, without official instructions of any kind. He also told me that Minvodkhoz and the Central Asian party organisations had tried to have it banned, but in vain.[13]

The commission's report argued that, quite apart from the cost, the environmental consequences of the project were incalculable and potentially very damaging, and the commission recommended abandoning the whole thing. Together with the appeal from the Writers' Union, this report seemed to catch the Politburo at a moment of critical indecision of the kind hypothesised by Gustafson. At any rate in August 1986 it ordered the suspension of all construction work, pending further study. It was not quite a conclusive victory for the ecologists, but it was nevertheless a remarkable success. Sergei Zalygin, chief editor of *Novyi mir*, and himself a hydraulic engineer by training, hailed the decision as the first ever major triumph of 'public opinion' over Gosplan and the industrial ministries.[14] It was certainly an indication of a sea change in the official attitude to the environment, and also in the capacity of writers and scientists to articulate views – or at least doubts and fears – hitherto widely held by people powerless to change anything.

It may be no accident that this decision followed quite closely on the explosion at Chernobyl', which demonstrated as no previous incident had the dangers inherent in allowing the economic leviathan to get out of control.

The explosion's full significance was dramatised two years later by one of the foremost architects of the Soviet nuclear power programme, Valerii Legasov, first deputy chairman of the Kurchatov Atomic Energy Institute. On the second anniversary of the explosion Legasov committed suicide, and in a *Pravda* article which was part suicide note, part testament, he called the disaster 'the apotheosis of the whole misguided way of running the economy which we had been pursuing for decades'.[15] By this he meant not only the secrecy – nuclear authorities everywhere are inclined to be secretive – but also the grandiose ambitions backed up by haste, wilfulness and slovenly workmanship.

The Soviet nuclear power programme was speeded up in the late seventies because of difficulties over other sources of energy. It promised to be clean, cheap and efficient, and it looked attractively 'modern', the sort of thing a self-respecting superpower could not afford to be without. In practice, however, it was often carried out, as most Soviet construction schemes are, with shoddy materials and to hurried schedules. Legasov was once horrified to find a welder failing to finish off the seams on a water cooling pipe properly, simply because he had so many seams to get through to complete his daily output target. The staff installed to run the stations were sometimes inadequately trained because the speeded-up building programme had left no time. Once the novelty of nuclear power had worn off, moreover, they got used to sloppy procedures and habits. As one station director once remarked to Legasov: 'What are you worried about? A nuclear reactor is only a samovar. It's much simpler than a thermal plant . . . Nothing will ever happen.'

This spirit seems to have underlain the fateful experiment which took place on the night of 25/26 April 1986. It was conducted in order to discover whether energy output could be continued even when the station was receiving very low levels of electric current from its own turbines, for example during a repair or a temporary power failure. We do not know why it was judged necessary to test this, but of course maximum output in all circumstances has always been a motto of the

Soviet economy, and Gorbachev had only recently made it clear at the 27th Party Congress that he was looking for *uskorenie* or 'acceleration'. (Is it merely my imagination, or has he used the word a lot less since Chernobyl'?) At any rate, since it was important to complete the test before the plant's imminent annual shutdown for repairs, the normal safety precautions (which might have accidentally aborted the experiment halfway through) were overridden. The result was that when a sudden increase in power unexpectedly took place, there was no way to prevent it surging into a full-scale nuclear explosion.[16]

Thereupon heroism mingled with duplicity and furtiveness in characteristic Soviet fashion. While firemen and technicians struggled self-sacrificingly (literally: some of them died) to bring the blaze under control, local officials tried to minimise what had happened and to localise information. Some of them even made hasty arrangements to evacuate their own families while leaving the public at large in the dark about the hazards. This obfuscation must have delayed Moscow's response to the crisis. Legasov first heard of 'some kind of accident at Chernobyl'' several hours before he was flown off to the site as member of an emergency commission, and even by the time he arrived he was quite unprepared for the scale of the disaster which lay before him.

The local population was needlessly exposed to presumably high levels of radiation (precise readings have never been disclosed) for up to a week after the explosion. The rest of the world heard about the disaster before those most closely affected, who had to pick up what they could from (sometimes exaggeratedly alarmist) western radio reports. Evacuation was begun belatedly, and some anxious parents besieged railway stations to try to get their children out of the danger zone.[17]

Faced with evidence that its customary minimal information policy was discrediting the Soviet Union abroad and sowing panic at home, the Soviet regime abruptly changed the policy, and started to put some beef into glasnost, which had hitherto existed on paper rather than in reality. It began to publish regularly updated information on radiation levels, monitored food supplies and advised on health precautions. It invited a commission of the International Atomic Energy Authority to come and inspect the disaster site.

Nevertheless, much uncertainty persisted and still persists. The public have remained worried that facts vital to their health were being withheld from them. This anxiety was intensified by the trial of officials from the power station in July 1987: foreign correspondents were excluded from most of the trial, and the impression was deliberately fostered that a few negligent officials were *entirely* responsible for the disaster. Questions of design, location, poor materials and bad workmanship in the construction of the station were neglected.[18] I myself recall a meeting held in the Ukrainian Writers' Union building in Kiev two years after the disaster, at which members of the public fired questions at officials about radioactive dust, the topsoil, the state of the rivers, and the safety of the 'sarcophagus' in which the stricken reactor had been encased. They evidently felt a good deal of scepticism and anxiety about the reassurances they were given.

With the lapse of time, in fact, public disquiet has not abated, but on the contrary been reinforced, both by official evasions and by further incidents at nuclear plants. In 1988 it seemed to reach a critical level. The publication of Legasov's testament undoubtedly contributed to this upsurge, as did Academician Sakharov's stated view that all future nuclear power stations should be built underground.[19]

An extreme view has been expressed by Ales' Adamovich, one of the leading writers of Belorussia, the republic which, because of the direction of the wind, suffered most from the early fall-out of the explosion. According to him, the real scale of the disaster was still being concealed from the public by the unholy alliance of three bureaucratic leviathans: Minenergo (the Energy Ministry, with powers similar to Minvodkhoz), solicitous of its nuclear power programme; Agroprom (the agricultural and food processing authority), straining to keep up its output figures; and Minzdrav (the Ministry of Health), eager to present a reassuring picture of a healthy population. 'All their efforts are bent towards concealment, not disclosure of the sources of danger. As they see it, atomic energy must be saved at all costs. Why, they've even invented the expressive word "radiophobia" to describe anyone who doesn't blindly put his faith in the specialists.'[20]

Adamovich's dig at the 'specialists' highlights a remarkable aspect of the recent public agitation over environmental matters: the loss of faith in 'specialists' and the assertion of the right of 'non-specialists' to express concern on matters which affect their lives. As Adamovich himself declared, 'I cannot afford not to take up matters which are "none of my business". I don't have the right not to. What specialists do, the results of their decisions, affect us all too closely.'[21] This is a novel sentiment in a society which has traditionally accorded almost unlimited respect to the 'men from the ministry' and taken a deferential view of science and learning. The strain of violating this deep-seated taboo may help to explain the somewhat hysterical tone of Adamovich's outburst.

Belatedly, then, concern over the consequences of Chernobyl' has built up into a broad questioning of the whole Soviet nuclear energy programme. The progress of the campaign is confusing to follow, since announcements that construction of a certain power station is being stopped are sometimes followed by further news that it is continuing. Perhaps there is an element of dissembling on the part of Minenergo, which after all has to find alternative employment for its workers or lay them off, which is almost unheard of. Departmental pride will not permit a ministry to admit to a shrinking work schedule.

Most of the protests over nuclear power have been in non-Russian republics, where environmental fears mingle with ethnic resentment in a way I shall return to in the next chapter. At the Kiev meeting which I alluded to earlier, many of those present seemed suspicious that the persistence with nuclear generation at Chernobyl' was in some way an attack on the Ukrainian nation. In Lithuania, after a fire in the Ignalina nuclear power station in September 1988, the Initiative Group in Support of Perestroika (embryo of Sajudis) organised a huge petition campaign calling for the station's closure and improvised a human chain of several thousand people round it. At about the same time, the Riga consultative meeting of non-Russian national democratic movements singled out the nuclear issue as one of especial concern: participants called the Soviet atomic energy programme 'a greater threat to European states than Soviet military might'.[22]

The upshot of all this public agitation was that by September 1988 an expert western observer felt able to remark that 'these protests have effectively made redundant the Soviet Union's ambitious programme for nuclear reactor construction to the year 2000'.[23] If so, this is an achievement even more remarkable than the prevention of the river diversion project. Of course it signifies no more than an uneasy stalemate, and Minenergo is probably reacting like Minvodkhoz, shelving the projects in the hope (or confidence?) of being able to resume them when more favourable weather returns. Besides, the stalling of nuclear power faces the Soviet Union with a potentially very serious energy shortage. Nevertheless, it seems clear that public organisations, inspired by writers and scientists, have proved themselves able to block, at least temporarily, vital components of the economic plan.

The growing public concern over the environment illustrates the way in which a potential constituency did exist for agitation over political problems, even when Soviet society, apart from a few human rights activists, seemed in a state of deep apathy. An analogous concern, widely felt but little expressed, was over the seemingly endless escalation of the international arms race, with its heedless consumption of resources and its threat to life on the planet. Now, an official Soviet Committee for the Protection of Peace did (and does) exist with the ostensible purpose of voicing this public concern, but few took its claims seriously, since, unlike western peace movements, it spoke in favour of a government which, by the late seventies, was the principal instigator of the arms race.

No unofficial peace movement arose on the western model until 1982, at a time when the long-established human rights movement was fading away or going underground. Then a circle of Moscow intellectuals set up a 'Group for Establishing Trust between the USSR and the USA'. Its first activity, a press conference held with western journalists, was very much in the spirit of the human rights movement: declarations of conscience using the western media to bypass the deaf-and-dumb

Soviet information channels. Before long, however, the Trust Group began to experiment with other means of reaching the Soviet public. It would hold seminars in private apartments on subjects such as the Soviet nuclear arsenal, the theory of non-violent action, or the conversion of the arms industry to peaceful purposes. It established contacts with visitors from western peace movements and used their materials to stage an exhibition on the consequences of the Hiroshima bomb and of children's paintings on peace. It was embarrassing for the security police to be seen removing exhibits so patently in accord with the ostensible policies of the Soviet government.

In the summer of 1984 the Trust Group transferred some of their action on to the streets of Moscow. On the Arbat, members collected signatures for a petition urging the Soviet and American leaders (Chernenko and Reagan, then in a relationship of glacial hostility) to hold a summit meeting as soon as possible. Passers-by proved less timid than was feared and, though surprised by an initiative which had no official approval, 300 gave their signatures in the two hours which passed before the police woke up to the fact that the action was unauthorised and rounded up the petitioners. In similar fashion in 1986 the group handed out leaflets in Gor'kii Park, providing facts about the Chernobyl' nuclear explosion, and passing on recommendations about precautions to be taken. It was carrying out a public service which the government had neglected, on a subject which caused most people deep and legitimate worries.

Participants in these and other public demonstrations were rewarded with brief spells in prison, and one or two of them with severer penalties, such as psychiatric detention and compulsory military service. But the resilience of the Trust Group showed that there were some prospects for a movement taking up causes which the Soviet government itself affected to support and using to the full the limited scope available for making contact with western colleagues and a wider Soviet public. The Group was feeling its way towards overcoming one of the major problems of the human rights movement – its relative isolation from the broad mass of the Soviet peoples.[24]

Another success of the Trust Group was its relative attractiveness to young people, anxious to do something practical about the serious problems affecting their society. Young people in the Soviet Union today are in a paradoxical and in some ways dispiriting situation. On the one hand their lives are materially more comfortable than those of their elders, and they have not been obliged to endure war, revolution or social upheaval. They are more educated and sophisticated, with a wider range of interests. On the other hand they are moving into a society which can offer them no obvious role. Whereas in earlier generations people gained interesting and responsible jobs on the basis of meagre educational attainment, the impressive qualifications held by some of today's young people are often not matched by the work they do. In fact their way is blocked by the *nomenklatura* appointments monopoly which installed their elders with life tenure. As Dr I. Il'insky, Director of Research at the Komsomol High School, has pointed out, demographic ageing has led to a reduction of the hiring of young people for administrative work, science and the arts. This both weakens their involvement in society and also limits their access to consumer goods, which often depends on professional position. Their civic maturation is slowed, and their sense of alienation intensified. [25]

Older people sometimes display a striking lack of understanding of their younger compatriots. Last year I talked to two writers in their fifties, men of real culture and human insight, who nevertheless assured me that today's young people, not having lived through serious deprivation and difficulty, were spiritually empty, and their literary attempts therefore insipid and lightweight. The Writers' Union, incidentally, is a classic instance of an official organisation unresponsive to youth: of its recent recruits only 20 per cent have been under 35 *at the age of entering.* [26]

The party's youth organisation, the Komsomol, is supposed to induct the young into this greying milieu, and so has naturally found itself in a classic 'piggy-in-the-middle' situation. Intended to reflect the aspirations of young people, it also has to convey to them an authoritative world view elaborated in quite different conditions and carrying little conviction today. Membership is not compulsory, but is more or less expected of young people with any ambitions in life. At least it was till very recently, but in 1988 Viktor Mironenko, its first secretary, revealed that membership had dropped by 10 per cent over the last three years, and that a quarter fewer 14- and 15-year-olds were joining it.[27]

The reasons for the decline are not far to seek. More than 50 per cent of the Komsomol's own members consider it bureaucratic and un-responsive to ideas from below.[28] Since about the mid-seventies, and in some cases even earlier, more and more young people have been taking things into their own hands, setting up their own voluntary associations and clubs to pursue all kinds of interests and aims, from basketball to yoga, rock music to international peace, breakdancing to environ-mental protection.[29]

Now Soviet law certainly permits voluntary associations, but it also demands that they register and attach themselves to a sponsor institution (RSFSR law of 10 July 1932). More enlightened or flexible Komsomol organisations come halfway to meet them, offering premises, advice and facilities. But not all voluntary associations have found sympathetic sponsors, and some of them have not bothered to register at all, meeting instead in members' flats or hiring premises wherever they could, in schools, palaces of culture, municipal buildings and so on.

Informal groups have been multiplying with remarkable speed. Early in 1988 it was reckoned that some 30,000 of them existed in the Soviet Union: today the estimate is 60,000. As many as 50 to 70 per cent of young people are estimated to belong to one or more, though the number of active participants may be much lower.[30] The range of their concerns is very broad, but perhaps half are in the field of culture or sport. About a tenth are estimated to be addressing political and social problems, while quite a large number of others are active in defending the natural environment or historical and cultural monuments.[31]

The great change since 1986 is that some groups of this kind have been encouraged by the official policy of glasnost to project their activities and ideas to a wider audience. The natural means by which they can achieve this broader publicity is by raising matters which arouse the concern of an educated and increasingly suspicious public: culture, the environment, history, ethnic and religious identity. The lively public response to them has in turn provoked a further increase in their numbers and in the vigour of their activity.

In Leningrad, for example, there has been for more than a decade a lively alternative culture, tacitly tolerated by the authorities. Its focus was the so-called Klub 81, which was allowed to hold poetry readings and even bring out an uncensored literary journal, provided its members circulated it strictly among themselves and did not seek western publication.[32] But the alternative groups sought a broader public only when early in 1987 the City Soviet announced that it was planning to demolish the Hotel Angleterre – distinguished, apart from its architecture, by the fact that the much-loved poet Esenin committed suicide there in 1925. Klub 81, together with other historical and ecological groups, collected signatures in the street for a petition to save the building. Partly by deception and partly by brute force, the city council cleared the demonstrators and moved their demolition workers in. The protesters then stationed an information kiosk on the square in front of St Isaac's Cathedral to hand out leaflets and answer questions. By this time nothing could save the hotel, but the activists drew from their failure the lesson – already long ago learnt by the human rights movement – that they must regard state and party as potential adversaries, and so must work together better in future and be more assiduous in seeking publicity.

Accordingly, they set up an umbrella organisation, the Cultural Democratic Movement, or Epicentre. Using the primitive technology of *samizdat*, Epicentre began to issue its own monthly journal, *Mercury*, carrying the watchword 'Claws and teeth for public opinion!' This contains open letters on cultural and environmental problems, as well as announcements of public discussions, lectures and meetings. Its editor, P. S. Filippov, set the tone in the first number: 'The activation of public opinion, its mobilisation as an effective instrument of perestroika – this is the main road which leads to socialist democracy.'[33] The spirit is very much that of Edmund Burke: 'When bad men combine, the good must associate; else they will fall, one by one, unpitied victims in a contemptible struggle.'

In Moscow, though there was no comparably dramatic event, the picture was similar: disparate groups of young concerned people doing their own thing and gradually being drawn together by the need for information, mutual aid and solidarity. The idea of a co-ordinating body first sprang from the apparently unpromising soil of the 'red corner' (communal meeting room) of a block of flats on the Arbat. In early 1986 a youth discussion group which regularly met there conceived the idea of an enabling group to help people with practical proposals for social work. They helped to launch a theatre studio, a computer club, and a building detachment to construct a home for the deaf and dumb. The official resistance they encountered to these projects raised broader political issues in their minds, and Gorbachev's calls for support from below emboldened them to establish a Club for Social Initiatives. Similar clubs arose at about the same time in Leningrad, Riga, Vil'nyus, Kaunas, Vinnitsa, Chelyabinsk and Novorossiisk.[34] They received the encouragement of the economist Tatyana Zaslavskaya (author of the famous Novosibirsk economic report of 1983) and of the Soviet Sociological Association, which, through its own Committee for Social Initiatives, was doing its best to regain some influence on social change, lost long ago under Brezhnev.[35]

According to its own charter, the Club for Social Initiatives aims 'to involve broad strata of the population in the process of self-government'. The activities it has sponsored are extremely diverse: helping the old and ill; preserving old buildings; sponsoring games for the disabled; holding seminars for workers on the recent 'self-administration' law; offering advice to people whose legal rights have been infringed; agitating for a monument to Stalin's victims; sponsoring discussion meetings on draft laws published in the Soviet press. Altogether, it was in danger of becoming Amnesty International, Greenpeace, Age Concern and the Citizens' Advice Bureau rolled into one. Accordingly, it has sensibly divided up, spawning sub-groups to specialise in particular problems:

one called 'Social Self-administration'; another, 'Civil Dignity', to advise and aid people who feel that their legal rights have been infringed; and the 'Philanthropic Society' to provide practical help for the old, ill or handicapped by shopping for them, cleaning their flats, or just talking with them. [36]

Sometimes political and social aims like these are married to a religious or philosophical orientation, like the Cosmos Club in Moscow, which combines the restoration of old buildings and international peace work with contemplative jogging in the Yoga spirit and shared meals which they begin with a joint meditation, imagining the mutual love that binds them to each other, to the city, the nation and the whole world. [37]

Some informal groups have emerged under the wing of official institutions, like the Perestroika Club, which originated in the Central Economic-Mathematical Institute in Moscow. It grew out of discussions on the new enterprise law held there in the spring of 1987, which brought together economists, sociologists, jurists, political scientists and others. The discussions were wide-ranging and spontaneous, and soon outgrew their original theme, raising issues which concerned the whole of Soviet society and attracting in the process a wider non-academic public. Some participants decided to move beyond discussion and set up action groups, each taking responsibility for a particular set of problems: one for legal rights, another for political questions, another for historical and cultural issues. One group, later called *Memorial*, set itself the task of arousing public concern for the building of a memorial to Stalin's victims – an aim eventually crowned with success at the 19th Party Conference.

But as the Perestroika Club grew politically more active, a symptomatic schism took place within its membership. This was between those who wanted it to act as a ginger group *within* the establishment, and those who felt it would be better to dissociate the club from existing authority structures and agitate from outside. In a nutshell, we have here the dilemma which confronts all informal activists in present-day Soviet conditions, a dilemma which in turn reflects the ambiguity of the current political scene, where a totalitarian party is proposing reforms which would end the totalitarian system. At any rate, the club split into Democratic Perestroika – more technocratic, strict about membership admissions, and in favour of working within the system; and Perestroika-88 – more libertarian, more open about membership, and less prepared to compromise with existing institutions. [38]

This kind of fracture may not be too damaging, since both sides seem to maintain good personal relationships – in contrast with the bitter splits of the nineteenth-century radicals. In the uncertain and ambiguous current situation, both modes of activism are probably fruitful in their own way. One view of the requisite strategy was put to me forcefully by Aleksandr Podrabinek, editor of the unofficial journal *Ekspress-Khronika*. If a cart is stuck in a bog, he said, then the best way to haul it out is not to wade into the mud, but to stand back from it, on firm ground, so as to have a reliable foothold. His own foothold is Orthodox Christianity, which he learned from Dostoevskii, and a belief in freedom and the rule of law as the basic preconditions for the existence of society. As he sees it, those who profess 'socialism' as the fundamental principle, or who hope to work through existing power structures, are merely slithering about in the mud and are likely to share the fate of the cart they are trying to extricate.

Ekspress-Khronika as a journal consciously moulds itself on the *Chronicle of Current Events*. In the late seventies Podrabinek edited an information bulletin on psychiatric abuse and wrote a book on the subject, *Punitive Medicine*, which was published in the west. For this he was charged with slandering the Soviet state and sentenced to five years' exile. Compared with the *Chronicle*, *Ekspress-Khronika* is much shorter and also much more frequent; otherwise its aim is exactly the same, dispassionately to record and publicise violations of human rights in the Soviet Union. Its editors meet every Saturday morning in a flat on the outskirts of Moscow, in the afternoon the typists get to work, usually going on far into the night, and on Sunday morning the journal is distributed on the Gogol Boulevard in the centre of the city. People come to pick up copies, pay what they can afford for them, and usually stay to ask questions. The police stand around in the background and watch, but usually do not interfere.[39]

An unofficial publication of this kind puts an immense strain on those involved. There are constant telephone calls to be answered, often from people distraught over what has happened to them, and their reports whenever possible must be checked. Typists and paper must be found, also couriers to distribute the final product – in spring 1988 *Ekspress-Khronika* was going to 53 towns, in 11 of which it was further typed and distributed. And all this must be done by people who have jobs of their own, and often families to look after in overcrowded apartments where books and papers seem to overflow from every shelf and table, and with technology which is utterly inadequate to the task.

The authorities' attitude to these unofficial journals is, as one would expect, ambivalent. They do not forcibly close them down, but on the other hand they decline to legalise them by official registration. Podrabinek, for example, was brushed off by the Moscow City Council with the comment: 'Your views on the freedom of the press are not consistent with Marxist-Leninist philosophy'. And Sergei Grigor'yants, editor of the unofficial journal *Glasnost*, was told by an official of the State Committee on Publishing that there was no need for new publications, since there already existed thousands of newspapers and periodicals, and besides there was a shortage of paper.[40]

At a meeting in October 1987 the editors of some thirty unofficial journals agreed that legal status was their most pressing need. As Podrabinek said: 'If we enjoyed the status of a co-operative, we could open a bank account, buy paper, rent premises, conclude a contract with a printing firm, have our own copying equipment.' They also requested 'open access to reprographic technology', which they called a prerequisite for genuine freedom of the press.[41]

Many informal political activists believe, unlike Podrabinek, that their place is in the mud alongside the cart, that unless someone puts his shoulder to the wheel, it will remain mired for ever. Those associations which are prepared to try to work with reforming elements in the party-state apparatus first came together in August 1987 at a conference in Moscow convened by the Club for Social Initiatives. Nearly 600 individuals from some 48 different groups participated. Most of them were of a 'broad left' persuasion, seeing Marx through the prism of Gramsci, Marcuse, the Yugoslav revisionists and the protagonists of the 1968 Prague Spring. They repudiated the Soviet version of 'real socialism', but did not disavow the idea of socialism altogether: they hoped to evolve a new version, responding to Gorbachev's calls for 'initiative from below' to develop links with ordinary people in their workplaces and homes and to prod the bureaucracy into more fruitful activity. They put particular emphasis on 'workplace democracy', on encouraging and helping workers to take advantage of their new rights under the 1987 enterprise law to participate in and monitor management decisions. At the same time, they rejected the methods of the human rights movement of the sixties and seventies as élitist, too remote from the interests of the masses. They also regarded with suspicion the market-oriented reform projects of economists like Aganbegyan, which they felt were likely to generate greater inequality, social injustice and probably unrest.

With so many groups represented, it is not surprising that many diverse views emerged at the congress. Not all groups could accept the majority consensus outlined above, and in the end two federations of informal political associations were formed, one of which (FSOK, the Federation of Socialist Clubs) required that its members acknowledge 'socialism' as their aim, while the other (KOI, or the Circle for Social Initiative) made no such insistence.[42]

The latter federation seems to have faded away, but the former has continued and extended its activities in an ambivalent relationship with the authorities. In January 1988 FSOK arranged a joint conference with the Komsomol, to see whether common ground could be discovered for permanent co-operation. However, when it became apparent that the Komsomol intended to swamp the conference with its members and to take over the agenda, FSOK withdrew and broke off contacts for a time, provoking a bitter attack in the Komsomol newspapers.[43]

The more democratic electoral system announced by the special 19th

Party Conference in July 1988 offered an opportunity for an alternative mode of coalition-building. During the summer FSOK joined with many other associations in trying to put together Popular Fronts in Support of Perestroika, with the aim of mobilising public backing for Gorbachev, especially among young people, against the conservative rump of the apparatus. This support, in the eyes of the movement's initiators, should not be uncritical: in fact, the Popular Fronts could be seen as performing many of the functions carried out in parliamentary systems by the official opposition.

Some of the more enterprising members of the Soviet legal establishment were evolving similar ideas. Professor Boris Kurashvili, of the Institute of the State and Law, for example, had formulated the theory that in a one-party system the competence and probity of the apparatus tends to degenerate unless someone is providing what he called 'social opposition'. Writing in a youth newspaper in April, Kurashvili proposed that Popular Fronts should monitor the work of government and party, criticise their legislative drafts, formulate alternatives, and keep data banks for the public to draw on for the purposes of informed discussion.[44]

It was perhaps natural that political groups endeavouring to play this kind of role should gravitate towards Boris El'tsin, former first secretary of the Moscow party organisation, who had been expelled from the Politburo in October 1987 for the intemperate manner in which he had upbraided his colleagues for not carrying through the reform process quickly or consistently enough.

The actual circumstances in which such Popular Fronts were founded often brought them into direct conflict with authorities who were inflexible or reluctant to tolerate criticism. An example of this kind was seen in Yaroslavl, where a Popular Front was formed at a public meeting on the bank of the Volga on 8 June 1988. It had been learned that the long-standing first secretary of the district party committee, one F. Loshchenkov, had been chosen as a delegate to the 19th Party Conference without any consultation with the rank-and-file party members. He was unpopular because he had encouraged the construction of a new chemical works in the town. The improvised meeting demanded Loshchenkov's recall and new elections, a demand to which the district party committee eventually acceded. Encouraged by their success, the initiative committee went on to organise weekly meetings in the football stadium, each of which would end by passing resolutions for action on local matters. In this way a Popular Front came into being, grudgingly tolerated by the authorities. When, however, the new Front wanted to publish its own programme – including open elections for leading public posts, and the abolition of privilege stores for *apparatchiks* – the local party newspaper refused to publish it. The editor told outraged leaders of the Front: 'I answer to the party. If they tell me to publish this, I will. But they haven't, so I won't.'[45]

The election campaign for the 19th Party Conference stimulated some lively provincial political activity of this kind. In Omsk an 'action group' comprising engineers, lecturers, students and Komsomol officials organised a rally in the Dynamo stadium one Sunday in May to discuss perestroika and to protest about 'the undemocratic nomination of candidates to the conference'.[46]

In the Urals industrial city of Sverdlovsk, popular opposition was aroused even earlier by the dismissal from the Politburo of their popular former first secretary, Boris El'tsin. An initiative group called Meeting-87 was set up at a public gathering. It brings out a lively journal, *Herald of the Urals* (*Ural'skii vestnik*), and has organised public meetings on subjects like 'The Democratisation of Soviet Society'. Ecological and Russian national groups have also been set up in the town.[47]

Their enthusiastic diversity makes the informal associations look at first sight a little frivolous or confused. But they should not be written off for that reason. This is a country where so much needs to be done. And since all political and social activity has hitherto been tightly controlled by the party, it is scarcely surprising that the first attempts at autonomous initiative should be disorganised and aim at too many targets. A lot of the institutional shaking out still has to take place.

Nevertheless, even in their present amorphous state, the informal political associations demonstrated in March 1989 in the elections to the Congress of People's Deputies that they had made a definite impact on public opinion. Although over the country at large the nominees of the apparatus were usually elected, the exceptions were both unexpected and conspicuous. In Leningrad, for example, Yurii Solovyov, first secretary of the regional party committee, and an alternate member of the CPSU Politburo, was defeated even though unopposed: so many voters crossed out his name on the voting slip that he failed to muster the 50 per cent required to go through. According to an eyewitness report, there had been demonstrations in the city, not directed against Solovyov personally, but simply bearing banners reading: 'If there is only one name on the list, cross it out!'

Local *nomenklatura* nominees were also defeated in Vladivostok, Khabarovsk, Kemerovo, Chita, Tyumen', Volgograd, Perm', Ivanovo and Kirov, in the Belorussian towns of Minsk, Gomel' and Mogilev, and the Ukrainian towns of Kiev, L'vov, Chernigov, Voroshilovgrad and Zakarpat'e. There is little evidence at the moment to suggest how many of these defeats resulted from the agitation of informal groups, but in Zhitomir, for example, a woman journalist, Alla Yaroshinskaya, won a remarkable victory after denouncing the privileges accorded to *apparatchiks*.[48]

A unique situation pertained in the Baltic republics, for there the Popular Fronts were no mere haphazard coalitions, but well organised mass movements (see next chapter). Candidates enjoying their backing won more than two-thirds of the seats; and the fate of the official candidate in those seats they did not contest was usually determined by whether or not they certified him as acceptable.[49]

Most sensational of all was the 90 per cent vote achieved in Moscow by Boris El'tsin against the party's official nominee. El'tsin's supporters in the Moscow Popular Front had organised public meetings for him in the Luzhniki stadium, attended by increasing numbers of inquisitive voters; and his popularity received a bracing pre-election boost when the party Central Committee announced it was going to investigate his 'breaches of party discipline'.[50]

Most observers were astonished at the results of the Congress elections. Of course, everyone knew that the public was bitterly resentful at the decades of misrule by the apparatus, the shortages of food, consumer goods and housing. But few expected the voters to register their discontent in such a concerted manner. The scale of the reformers' local victories – and also their very patchy distribution – suggests that the agitation of local informal associations, their posters, leaflets, public meetings and demonstrations, probably played a vital role in encouraging the voters, at least in certain regions, to articulate their feelings at the polling booths.

At the moment, state and party afford a measure of grudging toleration towards unofficial political initiatives. After all, Article 9 of the Soviet Constitution specifically states that the political system should evolve in the direction of 'greater involvement of citizens in the administration of state and society' and envisages 'increased activity of social organisations'. But the fact is that in the past all such organisations have been firmly under the supervision and, where necessary, ultimate control of the party. Gorbachev's opponents have warned that informal political associations encourage extremism and endanger the leading role of the party.[51] Gorbachev himself at the 19th Party Conference noted, on the whole with favour, 'the stormy growth of public associations reflecting all the diversity of social interests', and commented that 'under the one-party system we need a permanent mechanism for juxtaposing opinions, criticism and self-criticism'.[52] His remarks suggested that he hoped to weed out the few unacceptable *groupuscules* and absorb the rest into Popular Fronts.

Gorbachev may in theory acknowledge the need for citizens' initiatives generating oppositional activities, but he is not disposed to see an actual opposition arise, as was shown when some of the *neformaly* gathered in May to form a 'Democratic Union' as an unofficial opposition to the Communist Party: their meetings were constantly harassed by the police, though in keeping with the prevalent official ambivalence they were not actually prevented from forming their party and issuing a programme.[53] Many of their subsequent meetings have also been harassed. When, for example, they demonstrated on Pushkin Square in Moscow on 21 August 1988 to commemorate the twentieth anniversary of the Warsaw Pact invasion of Czechoslovakia, a hundred protesters were detained, and some forty subjected to fines or short jail terms. Some were apparently beaten up in the police station.[54] In keeping with the party's current ambivalence, however, their members have not been indicted for subversion, as would unquestionably have happened up to a year or two ago. Although under constant pressure, the Union has expanded, setting up branches in a number of cities in both Russia and the non-Russian republics: its political complexion varies between radical liberal and neo-Marxist.[55]

The proliferation of unofficial associations and journals suggests that Russians have lost none of their skill at improvising functioning human institutions under great pressure and stress. As I shall try to show in the next chapter, the same is true of other Soviet nations, some of which have the benefit of more recent democratic traditions. This does not mean that a western-style political system is about to appear, but it does mean that elements of a civil society are now in place. Their existence indicates that totalitarianism is in full retreat; if and when they feel secure and are able to operate normally, we shall be able to assert that totalitarianism has definitely ended. What is replacing it is a new kind of authoritarianism, in which the one-party system persists, but social stability, economic imperatives and the leaders' reluctance to resort to large-scale terror afford a certain guarantee against a relapse into tyranny.

5

The flawed melting pot

The national question in the Soviet Union provides a striking illustration of Tocqueville's celebrated dictum that 'the most dangerous moment for a bad government is when it seeks to mend its ways'. When Gorbachev came to power, it seemed not especially pressing. Though many non-Russian intellectuals resented in private – and occasionally in public – the domination of their culture from Moscow, their concerns appeared to outsiders esoteric, and it was not self-evident that their resentment was shared in any consistent fashion by workers and peasants. As for the local *apparatchiks*, though mostly indigenous, they owed their power, directly or indirectly, to the centre, and dispensed their loyalty accordingly. Despite sporadic outbursts of popular ethnic animosity, there did not seem to be a basis for asserting nationhood in opposition to Moscow. Above all, there were no autonomous associations to undertake the task.[1]

Yet a mere four years later, the picture is quite different. The resentful intellectuals have proved capable of mobilising the mass of their fellow countrymen. How can this be so? What has happened, I think, is that the factors which gave birth to informal associations in Russia have made themselves felt, with redoubled intensity, in the non-Russian areas. There issues of history, culture and the environment are even more salient, as symbols of national distinctiveness, and for the same reason writers and scholars enjoy a uniquely respected status. The whole dynamic of glasnost and democratisation has propelled ethnic factors to the centre of the Soviet political stage. That which totalitarianism repressed has surged powerfully to the fore, uniting people of disparate social backgrounds and career paths. An explosive realignment of loyalties and political structures has resulted.

The Soviet multi-national state is the last of the great European empires; and since the others have all fallen apart in the present century, it was in some ways to be expected that the Soviet one too should come under pressure from national liberation movements. However, things are not as simple as that. The Soviet Union is a decidedly unusual imperial entity. It resembles the Habsburg or Ottoman Empires, contiguous agglomerations of territory held together by military and administrative power. More than either of those, though, it is numerically and politically dominated by one nation, the Russians. But – and here the paradoxes start – that domination has not enabled the Russians to flourish economically, even by comparison with many of their ostensible 'colonies': compare, for example, the poverty of a village in central Russia with the relative prosperity of its counterpart in Estonia or Georgia. Nor indeed have the languages and cultures of the principal non-Russian peoples withered: in fact, in some ways they have developed and strengthened as a result of membership of the Soviet Union.

The truth is that this is not, in fact, in the normal sense a *Russian* empire. It is a Communist one, the first empire in history to be ruled over by a political party. From that fact flow the anomalies and contradictions of this unprecedented multi-national union.

The anomalies result from the unintended as well as the intended effects of the Bolshevik revolution. To take the intended effects first. Lenin held that classes, not nations, were the most fundamental social formations. Ultimately, he believed, nations would wither away along with states, and the proletariat would create an international community of peoples. In the short and medium term, however, he recognised that the national sentiment of Imperial Russia's subject peoples was a very useful ally in the struggle against the tsarist regime, and later in the civil war against the Whites. So before and during the revolution itself the Bolsheviks launched the slogan of 'national self-determination', supporting the emancipation of the subject peoples from Russia. In the immediate sense, the slogan was a great success: most of the non-Russians did ally themselves with the Reds and did gain some kind of independence, at least temporarily.

Once the Bolsheviks themselves were the masters, however, they inevitably took a much dimmer view of separatism, not only because they were the party in power, but also because theoretically they regarded 'national self-determination' as subordinate to the ultimate goal of 'proletarian internationalism'. During 1918–21 the Reds gradually and where necessary forcibly resumed control of most of the old Imperial Russian territories. Only Finland and Poland remained permanently independent, though it was 1939/40 before the Soviet Union could regain the Baltic region, eastern Moldavia and western areas of Belorussia and Ukraine.

So by 1922, when the Soviet Union as a political entity was finally formed, the way should theoretically have been open to introduce 'proletarian internationalism'. In practice, however, especially in the absence of socialist revolutions elsewhere, the Soviet state was not in a position to offer the non-Russians any kind of internationalism, proletarian or otherwise. The most it could extend to them was membership in a multi-national amalgam dominated demographically, linguistically and administratively by Russians. And this in turn was difficult to distinguish from actual Russification, the very evil against which the non-Russians had so recently fought, with explicit Bolshevik support.

This was the kind of 'proletarian internationalism' which Stalin favoured, but Lenin was well aware of the dangers. In the last years of his life he repeatedly warned of crude Russian chauvinism making its reappearance in the leather-jacketed breast of the Soviet commissar. He did not, though, have any political solution to the problem: indeed, the political structure he had instituted aggravated it. The Soviet Union was nominally designated a federal state, with considerable autonomy – and even the right of secession – granted to its constituent national republics. But in reality its administrative structure was highly centralised, with not only diplomatic and military power, but also economic power firmly located in Moscow. The Russian Republic (RSFSR), nominally just one of seven (later fifteen) republics, actually contained 90 per cent of the Soviet Union's territory and 72 per cent of its population. So it could scarcely help becoming the dominant member of the Union. Added to this was the fact that the Communist Party did not even *pretend* to federalism. Lenin always intended that power should reside unambiguously with the all-Union Central Committee in Moscow: the national communist parties of the constituent republics were, and have remained till very recently, no more than subordinate provincial units.

All the same, alongside this redoubtable concentration of political and economic power, a genuinely decentralised and pluralist approach to culture and education did prevail for a time. There were cogent reasons for this. Lenin had always believed that the political revolution needed to be complemented by a cultural one. He felt especially strongly about this when he surveyed the abject state of the country after the civil war. The Communists might be in power, but, as he saw it, they were not really running the country because they and most of the population lacked 'culture', that is, basic work habits and elementary notions of punctuality, probity and even literacy. Lenin hoped to overcome this lacuna by a crash programme of cultural propaganda, starting with the inculcation of basic literacy.

It made little sense to conduct such a programme in a language which people did not understand. So, like the medieval Catholic Church facing rural paganism, the party had to make use of local languages and show some consideration for inherited popular traditions. The twenties and early thirties saw the introduction of universal primary schooling in the various native languages, as well as the publication of books, journals and newspapers in the vernacular. In some cases this meant the revival of ancient cultures threatened with eclipse by the growing dominance of Russian under the tsars; in others it meant the transformation of what had been largely rural or tribal dialects into full-scale urban and literary languages with their own emergent high culture.

It is important to remember that not all ethnic communities survive into the modern world and become full nations. For every potential nation which makes it to nationhood there are a far greater number which fall by the wayside. Many dialects and folklores gradually fade away, or at least remain behind in the rural ghetto, when their bearers come to the city and are swamped by the broader, more sophisticated culture dominant there.[2] This was a fate which might, for example, reasonably have been expected to overtake the Ukrainian and Belorussian peoples in the early twentieth century. But Soviet nationality policy unintentionally ensured that this did not happen. If most Ukrainians coming into the towns during the Five Year Plans had been illiterate, then they would probably have acquired the habit of using Russian as an everyday language and would in effect have assimilated to Russian culture. Soviet education policy, however, ensured that they were mostly literate, and in Ukrainian. As a result, the towns became *more* Ukrainian during industrialisation. Whereas in 1926 65 per cent of Ukrainian town-dwellers named Ukrainian as their native language, in 1959, the next time the question was asked in a census, the proportion had grown to 77 per cent. In Belorussia the effect was even more marked, with a rise from 38 to 64 per cent.[3]

This movement of an ethnically aware rural population into the cities helped to lay the social base for the intensely nationally conscious intelligentsia of today. The effect was deepened by the elaborate administrative divisions of the Soviet Union, which gave even quite small ethnic groups their own miniature version of statehood in the form of an Autonomous Republic or an Autonomous Region. It was party policy that all such subdivisions should have their own indigenous cadres, that is to say, local nationals promoted through the *nomenklatura* ladder to hold high office in their own territory. These people were and are tightly supervised by representatives of Moscow in the party and the KGB, but they none the less symbolically embody the attributes of nationhood and have usually been able to act as powerbrokers on behalf of their ethnic colleagues.

Stalin, it is true, tried to re-establish a centralised Soviet hegemony with marked Russian nationalist overtones. Alarmed by the growing influence of these indigenous cadres, he purged them, accusing them of 'bourgeois nationalism'. He insisted on a Russian imperialist version of history being taught in schools, and was in the habit of referring to Russians as 'elder brothers' in the Soviet family. Worse than that, he tried to destroy some nations completely, by uprooting them and deporting them to distant and unfamiliar territories; or if they were too large, then he deported or murdered their élites, as he did in the Baltic, Belorussia and Ukraine in 1939–40. Yet never did he end the practice of conducting primary education in local languages, so that the nourishing of national feeling from below continued unbroken throughout his rule, irritated and intensified by his repressions and by the crude mixture of Marxism and Russian chauvinism which he imposed as cultural pap. Moreover, when in 1932 he introduced pass books, which all Soviet citizens had to carry, he included in them the category 'nationality'. A citizen's ethnic background thus became a permanent administrative fact, which would affect his fate every time he applied for education, a job or a residence permit. So whatever the official rhetoric about the ultimate merging of nationalities, their separate existence was authoritatively registered, with far-reaching consequences for everyday life.

All in all, the contradictions of Soviet policy have set the agenda for the conspicuous national revival which is going on today. Like other civic movements in the Soviet Union, this revival bears all the emotional force of the 'return of the repressed', the fervour of the sudden rediscovery of community amidst the rubble of the totalitarian heritage. The key role in this process has been played by writers and scholars, who are in a better position than most of their countrymen both to identify potential dangers and to articulate alarm at them. Whereas in the sixties and seventies such dissent did not often spread beyond limited circles, because the authorities used an array of sanctions to keep it within bounds, in the last two or three years various issues, different in each nation, have sparked off contact between these circles and a broader public which feels that its grievances are best encapsulated in ethnic demands.

The specific aspirations of each nation differ according to history and circumstance. For some the paramount concerns are territorial. It is easy to understand why: a nation without a homeland is deprived of the most elementary condition of community life. Already in the sixties, the Crimean Tartars, deported from their native soil by Stalin and forbidden to return by his successors, were able to mobilise most of their co-nationals for a mass campaign of demonstrations and petitions. The Jews are in an analogous condition: without a proper homeland in the Soviet Union, they saw an alternative one established in Israel in 1948. Feeling discriminated against in jobs, housing and education, they encapsulated their national aspirations in the demand for the right to *emigrate*, a desire little understood by other Soviet nations and easily dismissed as mere lack of patriotism.

The territorial issue which has most recently attracted the headlines is the Armenian demand to have the Autonomous Region of Nagornyi Karabakh incorporated into their republic. This is one of those emotionally overburdened problems whose implications are very difficult for outsiders to appreciate. The Armenians are an ancient people, one of the oldest Christian nations in the world, with much more than a mere millennium to celebrate. But for them territory and statehood have always been a sensitive issue, since for many centuries their population was uprooted and scattered between different empires. This has made them vulnerable to inter-communal violence, of which the Ottoman massacres of 1915 were only the worst example.

Nagornyi Karabakh is the easternmost area of Armenian settlement, a mainly pastoral and viticultural region. From a monastery within it the seventeenth-century Armenian Patriarch is said to have first written to the Russian tsar requesting protection against the infidel tyranny.[4] That is why the decision of 1921 to include Karabakh in the Azerbaijani Republic, with its Turkic population, has always deeply offended Armenians. The region was at that time more than 90 per cent Armenian in population, and the subjection to an alien race reminded them forcibly of the orphaned and vulnerable condition in which their people had so long lived.

Nor is it merely a matter of a historically based insult. In the one-party state, administrative subordination affects all aspects of life. Jobs, housing and economic development all depend ultimately on the Azerbaijani republican authorities in Baku, who tend to give preference to their own co-nationals over Armenians. Moreover, after four years of primary schooling, all parents must choose for their children whether to continue their education in Russian or in Azerbaijani, the language of the republic: Armenian is not an option.[5]

Armenians' loyalty to the Soviet state – which after all has remained their protector against hostile Muslim neighbours – long inhibited them from serious agitation to put the anomaly right. But they have made discreet representations about Karabakh, and even organised a street rally in 1974.[6]

Gorbachev's proclamation of glasnost encouraged the Armenians to raise the issue more publicly. In autumn 1987 they sent a petition with 75,000 signatures to the party Central Committee calling for the historical injustice of Karabakh to be rectified. They never received a proper reply. This tacit slighting of their claim coincided with agitation over another grievance which has figured frequently in recent ethnic protest, that of environmental damage. The air in the Armenian capital city of Erevan is so polluted by chemical factories that intellectuals sent an open letter to Gorbachev, talking of 'biological genocide' and citing a huge recent increase in cancer, cardiac and respiratory disease, and in birth defects.[7] The merging of these two streams of protest imparted the decisive mass appeal to the Armenian national movement. On 25 February 1988 a crowd estimated at between 500,000 and a million demonstrated in the streets of Erevan with banners proclaiming 'Karabakh is part of Armenia!' and 'Karabakh is a test case for perestroika!'[8]

The bursting of the genie from the bottle discredited the Armenian Communist Party, which had for decades acquiesced in both the territorial and the environmental affronts. The protests of 1988 were co-ordinated by a so-called Karabakh Committee, which according to the Soviet press was formed by writers, journalists and scholars, as well as officials acting in a private capacity.[9] It placed its branches in factories, offices and educational establishments – just like the Communist Party, and, practically speaking, in rivalry to it. It was in effect an unusually successful Popular Front facing a demoralised local Communist Party. The Armenian Supreme Soviet actually came down on its side against the party by voting for the incorporation of Nagornyi Karabakh.

Symptomatically, it was two writers, Sil'va Kaputikyan and Zorii Balayan, who were mandated to go to Moscow in March 1988 to lay before Gorbachev the concerns of the Armenian people. They returned to report that Gorbachev had promised them 'a new beginning' in Karabakh. He did not, however, honour this pledge in the sense in which they had understood it, by awarding Nagornyi Karabakh to the Armenian Republic. Presumably he feared a backlash among the Soviet Union's fifty million Muslims, and was reluctant to open the way to irredentist demands in other disputed border areas. The feeling of being let down naturally intensified Armenian bitterness. Apart from writers, the Armenian Church also began to play a more active role, with its head, Catholicos Vazgen, supporting the Armenian claim, but urging the people to behave responsibly and peacefully in pressing it.

In the end, after months of fruitlessly trying to ban the Karabakh Committee, Gorbachev took advantage of the earthquake of December 1988 to weaken it by arresting the eleven members of its Central Committee. Shortly after, he introduced direct rule from Moscow in Karabakh, supplemented by a virtual military occupation of the Armenian Republic.

The Azerbaijanis, not surprisingly, also regard the Karabakh issue as a test case for the ability of the Soviet Union to satisfy their national aspirations. They share with all Soviet peoples the sense that their economy and culture are not under their control, but are being alienated from them for someone else's benefit. The oil wealth of Baku is running out, having mostly been siphoned off to fuel the Soviet economy as a whole: the Azerbaijanis, as they see it, are left only with the pollution.[10] Their past culture has been placed at two removes from them by not one but *two* alphabet reforms. For them the Armenians are rich neighbours who have enjoyed an undue share of the Soviet Union's aggregate wealth: many of the better-off or more privileged citizens of Baku and Sumgait are Armenians. Doubtless such frustrations lie behind the appalling massacre in Sumgait, where a hundred or so Armenians were murdered in what seemed to many like a systematic fashion by their Azerbaijani neighbours.

In Georgia the Communist Party managed to retain more effective power for longer than in Armenia, but did not use it wisely, and has in the end suffered the same collapse of reputation as in the neighbouring republic. Like the Armenians, the Georgians are an ancient Christian people who have lived under constant external threat from expansive Muslim empires. In most other respects, though, their national experience has been very different from that of their neighbours. They had a great medieval kingdom, that of David the Builder and Queen Tamara, in which other small peoples were subject to their rule. Over the centuries that kingdom fragmented into petty principalities, and was only reunited under the Russian crown in the nineteenth century.[11]

Georgian national sentiment thus manifests itself in deep mistrust of outsiders, together with a fierce and anxious desire to hold together the nation's fissiparous territories and peoples. In that sense Georgia is a kind of microcosm of the Soviet Union as a whole.

This proud, militant patriotism is exemplified by Merab Kostava and Zviad Gamsakhurdia, in whose company I spent a number of memorable hours in April 1988. Gamsakhurdia's father, Konstantin, was a writer whose epic novel *David the Builder* chronicles the rise of the medieval kingdom. Zviad showed me his father's statue (significantly unnamed, for the Communist Party distrusts national heroes): he sits with stiff dignity, holding a curved sword at his knee. Sitting in a room austerely furnished but lined with books and prints, Zviad and Merab expounded to me in luxuriant detail the glories of their nation's history, and recounted their struggle, as leaders of the Il'ya Chavchadze Society (called after an early twentieth-century writer now thought to have been murdered by the Bolsheviks in 1908), in defending Georgia against peoples of the Baltic republics have the most recent memory of independence and of parliamentary democracy; and more than any other Soviet peoples they remained unreconciled to their incorporation into the Soviet Union. The experience of Stalin's brutality in the process of annexation in 1940 killed any positive support, even among most Communists, for rule from Moscow. A party leadership of nominal Balts (some barely able to speak their 'native' languages) had to co-exist with nations sullenly resentful of Soviet authority and determined to do their utmost to preserve their languages, customs and ways of life from external encroachment till a more favourable historical juncture. The Baltic became a discreet haven for experiments in the arts or in private economic enterprise which would not have been tolerated elsewhere.

In this soil a lively dissenting movement existed throughout the seventies, especially in Lithuania, where the disaffected Roman Catholic Church afforded it a semi-official shelter. In 1980, indeed, the Church succeeded in gathering no less than 148,000 signatures for a petition to have the closed cathedral in Klaipeda restored to believers: the largest petition, as far as I know, ever to have been presented in the Soviet Union up to that time.[16]

The Baltic peoples were, then, relatively well prepared for perestroika when it came. They have certainly been the most successful in taking advantage of it. Unlike the Armenians, they have not concentrated all their efforts on one overriding demand which Moscow cannot concede, but have chipped away at existing power relationships in a bewildering series of symbolic minor assaults. In the course of these, aspirations initially voiced only by dissenters were taken over first by scientists and cultural activists, then by broader public organisations, and finally – albeit hesitantly and incompletely – by the party itself. The pace differed somewhat in each republic, Estonia taking the lead, Latvia following closely behind, and Lithuania (less threatened in its national identity by foreign immigration) bringing up the rear.

As in the Caucasus, protests began over industrial projects, abhorred because they symbolised subordination to Moscow, because they degraded the environment, and because they brought in workers from outside to dilute the indigenous ethnic population. All of these concerns were felt especially keenly by Latvians, already a minority in their own republic. The plan to build a hydroelectric power station on the Daugava River, drowning an expanse of arable land and several villages, aroused opposition, first of all from writers, and then from a wider public writing in to the newspapers. 'Have those who sit in various Moscow planning institutes been but once to the places they so nonchalantly propose to obliterate?' asked one indignant correspondent, expressing the helpless rage of millions of Soviet citizens at their subjection to economic decisions taken far away and in complete ignorance of the people and places they would affect. 'For what will we use His Highness Electricity?' asked another no less pertinently. 'Perhaps so that the First of May factory can turn out a few more thousand defective pairs of shoes that no one will buy?' A petition campaign in 1986 eventually attracted 30,000 signatures, the republican party authorities supported the protests, and Gosplan in Moscow called off the project.[17]

This initial success encouraged further action. Under the weight of the injustices inflicted on them in the past, Baltic protest naturally takes up history as its theme. Gathering momentum throughout 1987 and 1988 demonstrations began to mark the fateful anniversaries: Independence Day; the day of the great deportations (14 June); the Nazi–Soviet Pact (23 August). Grimly enthusiastic crowds demanded full glasnost about these events, and a memorial to Stalin's victims.

Then came the stage of creating associations and formulating programmes. As in Russia itself, the preparations for the 19th Party Conference aided the process. In April 1988 secretaries of the Estonian cultural unions (representing writers, artists, musicians, etc.) drew up a comprehensive programme for the Conference condemning the local party first secretary, Karl Vaino, and denouncing the existing relationship between the Union and the constituent republics for generating 'an unprofitable economy, uncontrolled migration, increased risk of an ecological catastrophe, and failure to satisfy the population's social and cultural needs'.[18]

Taking their cue from this declaration, the plenum of the Writers'

Union in Latvia convened delegates from the other cultural unions in June, and dispatched an even more specific and radical programme. It asserted that political autonomy was required to ensure the bare survival of the Latvian people, now being swamped by immigrants in their own republic. They demanded that Latvia should become a sovereign state – still within the framework of the Soviet Union, though offstage voices were already demanding secession – with its own citizenship, its own seat at the United Nations (on the model of Ukraine and Belorussia) and its own military units with Latvian as the language of command. The republic would run its own economy, have the right to restrict immigration, and declare Latvian its sole official language.[19]

In spite of initial resistance, the Communist Parties of both Estonia and Latvia soon registered that this programme had the support of the overwhelming majority of the population, and that it would be prudent to compromise with it, in order both to avert an explosion and to head off more extreme demands. This was the motive for the party's support of the formation of a People's Front in Support of Perestroika, organised, like the party itself, with cells in both workplaces and residential areas. It brought together the cultural, scientific and technical intelligentsia with party officials and ordinary workers.[20]

Its programme declared at the outset that the USSR was a 'union of sovereign states', whose interrelations should be 'regulated by treaty'. Underlying this assertion was the tacit claim that the secret protocols of the Nazi–Soviet Pact, which had given Stalin *carte blanche* for the annexation of the Baltic republics, were invalid, since they had been agreed contrary to the norms of international behaviour and without the knowledge of the sovereign states affected. 'It is necessary to acknowledge officially that the annexation of the Latvian Republic to the USSR was carried out by force and without consulting the people of Latvia.'

Repudiation of the Stalinist past led naturally on to rejection of Stalinist politics. The programme nowhere made the expected obeisance to the 'leading role of the Communist Party': on the contrary, it envisaged the consolidation of 'socialist pluralism', such as would exclude 'the monopoly right of any political organisation to administer the state or social life'. Its constitutional recommendations were impeccably liberal, with complete separation of powers, a constitutional court, and guarantees of the full range of human rights. The most controversial points were the proposal to make Latvian the single official language, to terminate forthwith all immigration into the republic, and to establish the principle that Latvians should have a guaranteed majority in all local soviets within the republic, whatever the demographic situation in any given area.

The Popular Front programme said nothing (probably deliberately) about the conduct of foreign and military policy, and the demand for a separate Latvian army was toned down to 'the creation of a territorial military formation in which citizens of the Latvian SSR would discharge their obligatory military service, regardless of nationality'. This demand implied no more than the reintroduction of territorial units, which had been the norm in the Red Army up to 1938.[21]

To this forthright challenge the local Communist Parties, after some hesitation, reacted rather astutely. In Estonia, Vaino was dismissed and replaced by a first secretary more fluent in Estonian and more sympathetic to the aspirations of his fellow countrymen. Both Estonian and Latvian delegations adopted these Popular Front proposals as their official platform for the 19th Party Conference.[22]

In Lithuania events followed a similar course, if a little more haltingly. As late as August 1988, riot police were still turning out in force to disperse a demonstration being held in Vil'nyus's Gediminas Square to mark the anniversary of the Nazi–Soviet Pact. In the event, however, public indignation at this high-handedness was decisive in bringing about the downfall of the party first secretary, Ringaudas Songaila, replaced by the more acceptable Algirdas Brazauskas, who hastened to welcome the programme of the new Popular Front, known as Sajudis (the Movement).[23]

In all three republics the founding congresses of the People's Fronts, held during October 1988, turned into festivals of national rebirth. National flags, not displayed for nearly half a century, were once more hung from public buildings, anthems were sung by huge crowds, and in

Lithuania a packed service was held in the Roman Catholic cathedral which had been a picture gallery for forty years and was only just being reconsecrated. As one visiting journalist put it, 'the Lithuanians march back on to the map of Europe after 48 years of darkness'.[24]

Even as these celebrations were proceeding, however, counter-weights were being created. The non-indigenous (mainly Russian) population of the Baltic republics had initially displayed a remarkable degree of solidarity with the demands of their neighbours. By autumn, though, the prospect of having to deal with official documents in (say) Latvian became more real to Russians living in the Baltic. 'International fronts' or 'unity movements' began to spring up to protect the interests of the non-indigenous nationals. They protested against the planned restrictions on immigration and reasserted 'genuine bilingualism': the new language law, they declared, in effect instituted a *Berufsverbot* against Russian speakers. They warned that the republics were question-ing the leading role of the party and arrogating to themselves powers which undermined the constitutional integrity of the Soviet Union as a whole, and that this trend was encouraging 'extremists' intriguing to detach the Baltic from the Union altogether. They rejected what they feared would be a 'closed economy', and reaffirmed Latvia's need to trade within a federal market that would embrace the entire USSR.[25]

By the spring of 1989 the three 'Interfronts' were bringing quite large numbers of mostly Russian workers out on to the streets to parade with red hammer and sickle flags as symbols of devotion to the continued integrity of the Soviet Union. In March, for example, some 50,000 marched through Tallinn, protesting against 'creeping counter-revolution undermining socialism in Estonia': their banners read 'Down With Discrimination' and 'Give Russian the Status of an Official Language'. Strikes were threatened in the major utilities, to remind Estonians how dependent they were on their Russian working comrades.[26]

At the time of writing, serious violence has been avoided in the Baltic, partly because the local Communist Parties and the Popular Fronts have behaved in a moderate and statesmanlike fashion. Both sides seem content for the moment to allow the constitutional position of the Baltic republics to remain ambiguous. The Balts are now claiming that they remain members of the USSR by their own free and sovereign will: the Estonians, indeed, have explicitly asserted their right to veto legislation from Moscow which displeases them. For the time being, Moscow is contesting that interpretation only verbally. But if discontent among the Russians intensifies, or if violence breaks out, then Moscow may well decide to intervene with force. The principal danger, it seems to me, is that the opponents of decentralisation are likely to mobilise, probably in the form of an alliance between the more conservative *apparatchiks* and the Russian 'Ulster Unionists', who resent the appearance of discrimination against them in what they have become accustomed to regard as their own homeland. At any rate, by February 1989, the conflict between Sajudis and the Unity Movement so alarmed Brazauskas that he warned a plenum of the Lithuanian Communist Party's Central Committee that the republic might suffer the fate of Nagornyi Karabakh and be subjected to direct military rule from Moscow.[27]

The Baltic developments are worth following closely, since they may presage the future of the Soviet Union. After all, if Gorbachev's political and economic reforms work out according to plan, then the whole country will eventually look more like the Baltic today. The Balts are acting as pathfinders for perestroika: the Russians living there may become pioneers of the reaction against it.

Compared with the Baltic, the formation of Popular Fronts has encountered much more resistance from the Communist Party in Ukraine and Belorussia. There is good reason for this. The Ukrainians in particular occupy a key position in the constellation of Soviet nations. Whereas all the others are in some sense 'peripheral' – that is, geographically and economically they lie at the edge of the multi-national empire – Ukraine is 'central'. Without Ukraine, something is torn from the heart of the Soviet Union.

This is partly a matter of economics. Ukraine contains most of the fertile black-earth soil of European Russia: indeed, its abundant production once justified for it the sobriquet of 'granary of Europe'. Much of the extractive, metalworking and machine-building capacity which is vital to Soviet industry and the armed forces is situated there. It is also a matter of population. If it were independent, the Ukrainian Republic would be the largest nation in Eastern Europe apart from Russia itself. Furthermore, without the 42 million ethnic Ukrainians and the nine million Belorussians, the Russians number only one half of the Soviet population. Add them in, however, and the Russians become easily the dominant nation, numerically as well as politically. Since the Ukrainians and Belorussians are ethnically so closely related to them, moreover, the Russians have become accustomed to regard them more or less casually as co-nationals.

Rather like the English, the Russians have invested much of their ethnic awareness in the political structure they have created and sustained. They have, as a result, scant understanding for nations who possess no sovereign state of their own, and they expect Ukrainians and Belorussians to be content with the role of 'auxiliary Russians' in the vastnesses of the empire, in the same way that Englishmen would regard Scots as fellow-countrymen in the service of the crown. Russians tend to treat with good-natured but unmistakable disdain the idea that Ukrainians might be a separate nation: yes, they have their own picturesque customs and their own peasant dialect, but . . .

In some ways, Ukrainians' sense of their own nationhood is the mirror image of the Russians'. Historically speaking their own native aristocracy has been inclined to assimilate to whichever state happened to be dominant in their area at any given time: up to the seventeenth century the Polish, thereafter the Russian. By the early twentieth century, Ukraine could easily be seen as a potential nation which had failed to achieve full nationhood because its élites, its cities and its culture were dominated by others. But there is no doubt that the experience of independence in 1917–21, however beleaguered and precarious, followed by the cultural and educational flowering of the twenties, created a sense among all sectors of the population of belonging to a Ukrainian nation distinct from Russia. Many of the towns, into which newly literate peasants were streaming, became properly Ukrainian for the first time. The calamities which followed, the famine of 1932–4, the Stalinist purges, the Second World War and the German occupation, the partisan war against the Soviets, imparted to this national consciousness an embattled and heroic dimension. The Ukrainians have survived incredible adversities, some of them deliberately imposed by the Soviet government, and the heritage of 'blank spots' in their history is therefore a quite unusually sensitive one. [28] When I spoke to Ukrainian activists in the spring of 1988, I found them warm and outgoing as people, but imbued with a bitter sense that they had been betrayed, that their nation had deliberately been crippled.

This succession of renewal followed by repression underlies the remarkable upsurge of Ukrainian culture which took place in the late fifties and sixties, manifested especially in the poets who are today referred to as the 'sixties generation'. It also explains the response of the Soviet authorities, which has been more consistently repressive in Ukraine than perhaps anywhere else. Two great waves of arrests, in 1965 and 1972, engulfed those who sought Ukrainian independence, or even merely a greater degree of autonomy within a Soviet federation. Furthermore, under Gorbachev, long after personnel changes had shaken the leadership in all other union republics, Ukraine was still ruled by a Brezhnev appointee, Shcherbitskii, and repressive vigilance, though more sporadically applied, was still felt as an omnipresent threat. As a joker put it to me in 1988, 'You want a rest from perestroika? Then come to Ukraine!'

There exist more subtle and enervating dangers to Ukrainian nationhood than those directly posed by the authorities. Principal among them is the question of language tuition in schools. Since 1959 it has no longer been compulsory to teach a child's native language; the teaching of Russian, however, remains compulsory, and is vigorously promoted throughout the Soviet Union. This has weakened the position of non-Russian languages everywhere, but it has especially affected Ukrainian, because of its closeness to Russian. The problem is that, given the choice (as by law they must be) many parents will send their children to Russian-language schools, or at least to mixed-language schools where Russian is in practice usually dominant. The reason for this is clear. Children who are used to thinking and speaking in Russian find it easier to get into higher education and then to take up jobs outside their native republic. In practice, too, they will often find it easier and more convenient even within Ukraine to conduct their affairs in the imperial language. The result is that the number of Ukrainian-language schools, where Russian is taught only as a second language, has been declining sharply. Today in Kiev, the capital of the Ukrainian Republic, only 34 out of 274 schools (12 per cent) are Ukrainian, while 152 (55 per cent) are Russian.[29] This decline means that gradually Ukrainian is becoming a purely domestic and family language, while Russian is increasingly taken for granted as the natural medium for all public affairs, as well as for scholarship and culture.

In 1987 the Ukrainian Writers' Union took up the gradual atrophy of their language as a public cause. At a plenary meeting in June Dmytro Pavlychko warned that, if things went on as at present, the Ukrainian language 'would probably survive only in Canada'. He proposed a law making study of the language, literature and history of any republic compulsory in all its schools, including Russian ones. He also recommended that the republican Minister of Education, rather than parents, should have the power to decide any school's language of tuition.[30] A situation has been reached where Ukrainian patriots feel obliged to erect a defensive rampart round their vulnerable culture.

Ecological grievances have been gradually gathering momentum for many years because of the concentration of heavy industry and the growing use of intensive agricultural methods in Ukraine. They were brought to a head by the explosion in the nuclear power station at Chernobyl' in April 1986. Writers and scientists joined hands to protest at the evils which this disaster uncovered, the 'diktat of producer over consumer' and the practice of taking decisions deeply affecting local people's lives without even informing them, let alone consulting them. The Writers' Union set up an Ecological Commission to monitor the situation, and the pages of its weekly newspaper *Literaturna Ukraina* became the best source of information in a press which, for the most part, remained dully conformist.[31]

I myself attended a meeting on the second anniversary of Chernobyl', organised by the Writers' Union and chaired by a writer, Yurii Shcherbak, who has written a novel about Chernobyl'. It was attended by several hundred people crowded into a modest-sized hall in the Union's Scottish baronial mansion just off the main street of Kiev. Here for three hours writers and members of the public cross-questioned officials of the Ukrainian Energy Ministry about radiation hazards, evacuation procedures, the pollution of rivers and agricultural land. The atmosphere was boisterous, though not disrespectful, and deeply sceptical. Meanwhile a demonstration was taking place in the main square not far away, with young people displaying placards calling for the closure of all nuclear power stations in Ukraine. It was swiftly broken up by police and the demonstrators were bundled into buses. A woman whose son had been arrested came to the writers' meeting and challenged them: 'You writers are the conscience of the people: it is up to you to do something to help those detained.' Reaction to her was mixed, some in the audience evidently feeling that public demonstrations were not the best method of dealing with a complex problem like nuclear energy.

The organisers of that demonstration were the Ukrainian Culturological Club, which has been at the vanguard of the unofficial public movement in Ukraine. Set up in August 1987, it has continued the work of the Ukrainian Helsinki Group of the seventies, bringing out a *samizdat* journal, *Ukrains'kii Visnik (The Ukrainian Herald)*, and organising public meetings on ecology, historical monuments, culture and on the 'blank spots' of recent history. They have sponsored, for example, a memorial gathering for Vasyl' Stus, one of the leading sixties generation poets, who died in a labour camp in 1985; and they have organised evenings of testimony and discussion on the famine of 1932–4. The Culturological Society is far from being the only informal association to promote awareness of Ukrainian language, culture and history: the Hromada (Community) Society at Kiev University, the Lion Society in L'vov (called after the name of the city) and the Ukrainian

Helsinki Association (monitoring the treatment of political prisoners) are further examples. [32]

The Ukrainian informal associations have experienced much more difficulty than their Baltic counterparts in creating a Popular Front. When they first tried to do so in summer 1988, the authorities forbade meetings and detained known activists, even driving some of them out of town and dumping them in the countryside on the days of planned occasions. [33]

The turning point came, as in so many national republics, with a big meeting on ecological issues, held in Kiev. Ten thousand people gathered in Kiev Stadium in freezing weather on 13 November. The authorities permitted the assembly, but insisted on the removal of placards saying 'Hiroshima, Nagasaki, Chernobyl'' and even 'A Nuclear free Ukraine'. Dmytro Pavlychko, Yurii Shcherbak and others called for the establishment of a Popular Front, and on 4 December an Initiative Group met, including representatives of the Writers' Union and many of the informal associations. [34]

The programme of the Popular Front was at last published in the Ukrainian Writers' Union weekly (presumably the only paper that would carry it) in February 1989. It was similar to the equivalent Baltic documents, expressing support for the Communist Party's programme of perestroika, and calling for 'genuine sovereignty for Ukraine', the full range of human rights, a self-managed economy and 'the granting of the status of state language in the Ukrainian SSR to Ukrainian'. 'The practice of parental free choice in the language of education . . . leads', it warned, 'to national nihilism.' [35]

No sooner had this programme appeared than a riposte was published in the organ of the Ukrainian Communist Party, signed by a number of scholars in the Ukrainian Academy of Sciences. They dismissed the Popular Front as no more than an 'initiative group of the Kiev branch of the Writers' Union', and attacked it for trying to drive a wedge between the party and the people and for denying parents' constitutional right to choose the language in which their children should be educated. [36] One imagines that it will be possible in Ukraine to mobilise a substantial number of Russians and other non-Ukrainians in this way, by emphasising the unity of the Soviet Union and the right to continue using the Russian language.

In Belorussia, too, the formation of a Popular Front encountered determined opposition from the republican Communist Party. Much of the impetus for the expression of national feeling derived from the discovery of a mass grave of Stalin's victims in the Kurapaty Woods outside Minsk, the Belorussian capital. An informal society called 'Martyrology' was set up to promote the idea of a memorial and to call for a public commission to carry out an independent investigation of Stalin's crimes in Belorussia. This led on to the idea of a Popular Front to articulate the Belorussian national interest over the whole range of politics. As ever, scholars and writers were in the forefront of the movement, notably Belorussia's leading writer, Vasyl' Bykau. So too were the patriotic youth associations, Talaka (the Belorussian word for a peasant community) and Tuteishya (People from Here).

When these groups held an anti-Stalin demonstration in Minsk on 30 October 1988, the authorities sent in riot police with truncheons, tear gas and water cannon to disperse it. This outrage prompted Bykau to write an article of protest in the Moscow magazine *Ogonyok*, and the Belorussian Writers' Union announced that it would receive signatures from those who wished to register as members of the 'Renewal' Popular Front. The programme of the new movement, which is very similar to that of its Ukrainian counterpart, has not, as far as I know, been published in the republic's press. [37]

One intriguing development in Belorussia is that, in the face of official refusal to rent them a hall, the unofficial groups promoting a Popular Front held one of their meetings in premises provided free of charge by Sajudis in Vil'nyus. The Belorussians are closely linked by their history with Lithuania, but this is only the most conspicuous example of a growing willingness among non-Russian national movements to work together. A co-ordinating committee was set up in June 1988, representing the national movements of Armenia, Georgia, Ukraine, Lithuania, Latvia and Estonia. It issued declarations in September, some of which were addressed to the signatories of the Helsinki Final Act and expressed concern about political prisoners, about the Soviet nuclear power industry, and about the authorities' continued failure to satisfy the national aspirations of the Crimean Tartars and the Armenians in Nagornyi Karabakh.[38]

Conspicuous by their absence were the Russians and the Muslim nations. The Muslims are presumably distrustful of *all* Europeans, especially perhaps the Armenians, and so (except for the Crimean Tartars) are not prepared to work with them. The Russians, however, were absent either because they did not appreciate the importance of the national liberation movements within the Soviet Union, or because they were opposed to them.

When the non-Russian co-ordinating committee met again in January 1989 (joined by representatives of the Belorussians and Crimean Tartars) it addressed an appeal 'to the Russian Intelligentsia', warning: 'Many of the activists of the Russian democratic opposition have not yet grasped the primary axiom of democracy: nations cannot be free if they oppress others, or if they serve as instruments of such oppression.'[39] They are, I believe, justified in this reproach. With few exceptions (one of whom is Solzhenitsyn, in Vermont), the Russians have not yet realised that they have a common interest with the non-Russians in resisting a totalitarian apparatus which has oppressed them all.

In the Central Asian republics Brezhnev's benign policy of 'stability of cadres' permitted the entrenchment of local party leaders adept at achieving a *modus vivendi* with local communities. In the year of Brezhnev's death, 1982, four out of the five republican first secretaries (those of Uzbekistan, Kazakhstan, Kirghizia and Tadjikistan) had been in office for twenty years or more, while the exception (the first secretary of Turkmenia) had already lasted thirteen years. During this time they had used the *nomenklatura* system to build up networks of patronage, promoting their own acquaintances, local favourites or extended families, while keeping Moscow happy by reporting impressive figures for the learning of Russian and the output of cotton. They also became increasingly tolerant of Islam (see next chapter).

Over the years, old-style nepotism combined with the chicaneries of the planned economy to generate a formidable edifice of corruption which some have compared to the Mafia. Embezzling funds from Moscow by exaggerating cotton production figures, local party leaders used the proceeds to stimulate whole branches of the 'black economy', to remedy shortages of goods and services, and to provide lucrative jobs for favourites. If the state procuracy got wind of these operations, it took no action, for, as a later investigation explained, 'everything was excused and camouflaged by traditional hospitality and the need to fulfil the plan'.[40] Russians living in the Central Asian republics were generally excluded from these arrangements, except where they needed to be bribed, and so felt discriminated against or even victimised.[41]

Although the region was kept quiet by this tolerated particularism, its results were quite damaging to the Soviet system as a whole. It contributed less than nothing to the *rapprochement* of the Soviet nations which was the official policy of the CPSU. On the contrary, the censuses of 1970 and 1979 showed that intermarriage and the settlement of outsiders in Central Asia were beginning to decline, while Central Asians themselves were becoming extremely reluctant to quit the relative security of ethnic protectionism to take up jobs going begging in other parts of the Soviet Union. Besides, the rapacious use of water for the irrigation of cotton plantations was drying up the Amu-Darya and Syr-Darya rivers, lowering the water level of the Aral Sea and causing it to shrink by more than a half. The rapid encroachment of salty marsh and even desert on its banks endangered the public's supply of drinking water and threatened to alter the whole climate of the region, creating hotter summers and shorter winters, and jeopardising the whole cultivation of the cotton for which the irrigation had been undertaken in the first place. One Uzbek writer, visiting a fishing village which used to sit astride a neck of land with fishing boats moored on both sides, wrote that now desert stretched out in all directions as far as the eye could see. The Central Asian party leaders had been hoping to stave off disaster by receiving water diverted from the north-flowing rivers of Siberia, but this project was, as we have seen, cancelled in 1986.[42]

Moscow's attempt to regain control of the region began under Andropov in 1983, when a special investigation team was sent to Uzbekistan. Among other things it precipitated the fatal heart attack of Sharif Rashidov, party first secretary there since 1959, who was soon shown up as a past master of the skills needed to run a semi-criminal barony. By the end of 1986 all five republican secretaries had been replaced, and criminal proceedings had been set in motion against their subordinates. What the investigations disclosed may be exemplified by the case of one Uzbek state farm director, a certain Adylov, who had turned himself into a local tycoon, maintaining several luxurious villas, stocked with racehorses and concubines. He loved to sit on a granite podium by a fountain at one of his villas, under a statue of Lenin raising his arm as if in blessing: there Adylov would sip Napoleon brandy, issue his orders, hand out reprimands, and, if the mood took him, have recalcitrant vassals whipped.[43]

The procuratorial investigations in Uzbekistan have proved very sticky. It is not clear whether the main explanation for this is obstruction by local officials and underground businessmen beholden to the old regime, or widespread popular resentment at external interference in local affairs. One reason for the difficulties was revealed when the man sent in as Rashidov's successor to clean up the show, Inamzhon Usmankhodzhaev, abruptly resigned in January 1988 and was himself subjected to criminal charges. The trial for corruption of Brezhnev's son-in-law, Yurii Churbanov, also prompted a string of further press revelations about the Uzbek mafia.[44]

The first open resistance to outside intervention came, however, in Kazakhstan, when Dinmukhamed Kunaev, party first secretary, was replaced in December 1986 by a Russian, Gennadii Kolbin. This was an exceptional violation of the custom that republican first secretary-ships should be held by a member of the indigenous nation. Why Gorbachev overrode local susceptibilities in this conspicuous manner is not clear: perhaps he could find no suitably qualified Kazakh who could be trusted to root out corruption. At any rate the affront provoked two days of rioting in the Kazakh capital, Alma Ata, when a student demonstration apparently got out of hand. Students are probably the most nationally conscious element of the whole Kazakh population, and, being system-atically preferred over Russians in admission to college, had the most to lose from the undermining of existing ethnic protectionism.[45]

In June 1989 a problem left by Stalin erupted into a savage outburst of ethnic violence. Uzbek youths in half a dozen towns attacked the homes of Meskhetian Muslims from the Caucasus, who had been deported there in 1944 and never permitted to return home. The combination of a high Central Asian birth rate with economic uncertainty, aggravated by the abandonment of the Siberian rivers diversion project, had intensified the competition for jobs and official favours, and revived old resentments among Uzbeks about having an alien people dumped in their midst. The violence was unleashed by a dispute over the price of strawberries in a local market: it exemplified the way in which economic and ethnic resentments can easily become superimposed on one another. In the end special MVD troops had to be flown in to restore control over pogroms in which a hundred or so people are said to have lost their lives.[46]

While conducting old feuds and maintaining, even extending, semi-feudal social institutions, the Central Asian peoples have been strikingly slow to create civic associations of a more modern type such as have emerged in most other regions of the Soviet Union. Where such associations have made their appearance, they have been stimulated by writers and scholars as the individuals most likely to have contacts outside Central Asia. But at the time of writing it is too early to say how, or whether, they will develop.[47]

One possibility is that popular ethnic feeling tends to focus round Islam (which I look at in the next chapter) rather than around political demands of the type advanced by Popular Fronts. Another unknown factor which will affect Central Asia is the fate of the People's Republic of Afghanistan just across the border. The success of the mujahedin there, especially in the face of a Soviet-backed government, might inflame ethnic feeling, especially among the Tadjiks. But one can say with confidence that any systematic attempt to make the inhabitants of the region conform to Muscovite norms will continue to encounter at least passive and possibly violent resistance. At the same time, economic reform as envisaged by Gorbachev may actually strengthen hitherto illegal or unofficial sectors and thus intensify discrimination against Russians. Moreover, the absence of any discernible solution for the growing ecological problems of the region is likely to increase discontent.

One nation in the Soviet confraternity is in a very singular position, and that is the Russians. They are to all appearances the imperial nation, the 'elder brother', in Stalin's words. They have no worries about their territory, or language, or alien immigration: in fact, other nations feel threatened by *them*. Yet, curiously enough, in some respects the Russians feel like a national minority discriminated against in their own country. They know that the non-Russians are often more prosperous. And they can see that since 1917 their church has been undermined, their rural way of life mortally enfeebled, their finest writers, artists and thinkers banned, driven into the underground and emigration.

As an imperial nation, the Russians, like the English, tend to invest their ethnic consciousness in the state structures they have created. But what happens when those structures turn round and victimise Russians? Whom are they to blame for that? Actually it was the Communist Party, especially but not only in its Stalinist guise, which inflicted these injuries, but not all Russians have the detachment to appreciate that fact. And since there is no ethnic 'elder brother' to reproach, it is easier to heap imprecations on the Communist Party's traditional targets, on international imperialism and on unspecified 'rootless cosmopolitans', which usually means the Jews.

The advent of perestroika has in many ways intensified the paradoxes of Russian national consciousness. The vague and brooding sense of being victimised has been much sharpened both by the revelations of glasnost and by the surge of national liberation movements in the non-Russian republics. Conflict is most acute in the Baltic, where, in reaction to the self-assertion of the Estonians, Latvians and Lithuanians, 'unity' movements or 'international fronts' have been created to protect the interests of non-local nationals. The driving force in these movements probably consists of Russians suddenly faced with the prospect of having to learn (say) Estonian in the next few years in order to cope with everyday life. They have protested against planned restrictions on immigration and have asked for legislation granting supremacy to local languages to be suspended, and genuine bilingualism to be consolidated. They have warned that the Republican Supreme Soviets, especially in Estonia, are arrogating to themselves powers which call into question the constitutional integrity of the Soviet Union; and that the situation is encouraging extremists who are intriguing to detach the Baltic republics from the Union altogether.[48]

This warning casts the shadow of what I believe may well prove to be the most serious threat to the whole of perestroika, certainly in the form which it assumed during 1987–8: that is, an alliance between the Communist Party's conservative *apparatchiks* and a militant Russian nationalism spearheaded by the beleaguered Russians living in the non-Russian republics.

In the last couple of years an informal association has also arisen inside Russia itself to articulate the sentiments of Russians who feel threatened by the separatist forces which perestroika has unleashed. Known as Pamyat' – Memory – it originated, like its non-Russian counterparts, as an action group of those concerned about the protection of the environment and historical monuments. Some say it was founded by V. Chivilikhin, the writer who first raised the alarm about the pollution of Lake Baikal. Whatever its origins, it has broken far away from them.

In many ways, we are poorly informed about Pamyat'. We know next to nothing about its numbers, its membership or its organisation. We have accounts of its members parading at times in black shirts, embroidered with a bell, the symbol of the ancient Russian *veche*, the folk assembly. Its manifesto poses assertively the questions which bother many Russians: 'Who has defiled our history and culture? Who has been undermining our economy and destroying our agriculture all this time? Who has been destroying the nation with ideological and alcoholic drugs?' Its answer is 'the cosmopolitans', and it warns that 'international imperialism, sustained by Zionism and by its servile, mercenary lackey, Freemasonry, is attempting to plunge the world into the vortex of a new global catastrophe'. Among its enemies it identifies prominent reformers, like Aganbegyan, Zaslavskaya, Vitalii Korotich (editor of *Ogonyok*) and Aleksandr Yakovlev (Gorbachev's principal ideological adviser).[19] To such people it sends threatening letters: 'We shall get even with you. Signed: warriors of the patriotic union Pamyat'.'[50]

An Italian who chanced across a Pamyat' meeting in Leningrad commented: 'A whole week has passed, but I haven't shaken off the feeling of horror. I felt as if I were attending a real Fascist meeting of the 1930s.'[51] Although its programme also contains unobjectionable demands, such as freedom of speech, temperance and the revival of the Orthodox Church, its language and methods leave no doubt that this judgement is essentially correct. Pamyat' represents a throwback to the sentiments cultivated by Stalin in his last years, anti-imperialism, Russian chauvinism and anti-Semitism, now reawakened by the unfamiliar and unsettling conflicts of perestroika.

This would make it the natural ally of the conservative wing of the party-state apparatus, of those who have most to lose by perestroika. Such an alliance would be nothing new. Ever since the thirties the Soviet Communist Party has sometimes made use of Russian nationalism as an auxiliary ideological force with more mass appeal than Marxism.[52] In the turmoil generated by perestroika it may be tempted to do so again now.

For the moment, however, the signs are that Pamyat' is not considered respectable enough for such august fraternisation. Its meetings proceed relatively unimpeded – compared with those of, say, the Democratic Union – which indicates that there is a degree of official support for it. But it is not given space in the Soviet press, probably justifiably, since some of its utterances would fall foul of the law prohibiting the propaganda of racial hatred.

The more 'respectable' face of Russian nationalism, and one with considerable political potential, is the Writers' Union of the RSFSR.

The writers and journals grouped round this organisation can by no means be dismissed as Stalinist, chauvinistic or demagogic. During the 1970s, indeed, *Nash sovremennik*, the most successful of the Russian national journals, took the lead in exposing Stalin's crimes, and especially the brutal collectivisation of agriculture, in a manner which anticipated (though it fell far short of) the revelations stimulated by recent glasnost. Some of its leading authors, like Sergei Zalygin and Vasilii Belov, had originally made their name in Tvardovskii's *Novyi mir*, and they continued his tradition of truthful investigation of the life of ordinary people, especially peasants, throughout the upheavals of Soviet history.

In the spring of 1988 I had the opportunity to interview Sergei Vikulov, the chief editor of *Nash sovremennik*, who is a vigorous and forthright, sometimes even overbearing man. He told me how, on taking over the journal in 1968, he had decided not to try and attract the fashionable intelligentsia of the capital city, but rather to back writers from the Russian provinces. He claimed that Tvardovskii himself, after leaving *Novyi mir* in 1970, had encouraged his former protégés to go over to Vikulov.[53] At any rate, the move was an astute and fortunate one, and *Nash sovremennik* became the most interesting literary journal of the seventies, specialising in the 'village prose' school of writing.

To understand its orientation, one must appreciate that there is more than one kind of Russian national consciousness. To polarise the various sub-species somewhat, one may say that at one extremity there are the National Bolsheviks, those who see the Communist Party and the Soviet state as the best guarantors of the integrity of the Russian Empire and the continuity of Russian national traditions: such people tend to be atheists, and to worship Stalin as a hero. At the other pole are the 'revivalists', those who care most about Russian culture, the Orthodox Church and the way of life of the peasant village; they are usually Orthodox believers, and they execrate Stalin as the destroyer of that culture. In the era of glasnost they are moving closer to expressing their doubts not just about Stalin, but about the October revolution and the whole Communist enterprise as forces which have undermined the Russian national essence.[54]

As a result of the efforts of the revivalists, something of a *Historiker-streit* is developing in the Soviet Union – though characteristically not among historians, but among writers and critics – which might in the end become more important than its analogue in West Germany. Some of the participants in the controversy feel that the revelations of the glasnost era, by concentrating so much on the crimes of Stalin, fail to penetrate to the fundamental causes of the Soviet Union's problems. The point at issue was dramatised by the writer Vladimir Soloukhin late in 1988, when he refused to sign a letter calling for a worthy memorial to the victims of Stalin's purges. The motive for his refusal, he explained, was not sympathy for Stalin, but rather the absence of any answer from *Memorial* to his question 'From which year must we consider repressions illegal and unjustified, and up to which year should we consider them legal and justified?' What about the millions of victims of the forced collectivisation and 'dekulakisation'? What indeed about the lawless mass killings of the Cheka in the very earliest years of the Communist regime, when (although Soloukhin did not mention it) Lenin was still heading it?[55]

The critic Vadim Kozhinov made the same point on a broader scale when reviewing Anatolii Rybakov's novel *Children of the Arbat*, whose subject is the lead-up to the murder of Kirov in 1934. Kozhinov reproaches Rybakov with placing all the blame for the evils of Soviet society on Stalin and a clique of close advisers. He points out the enormous population losses of the years 1917–35, before the start of the famous 'purges', and, like Soloukhin, dwells on the suffering of the peasantry. Lenin, he reminds his readers, made no secret of his belief that the dictatorship of the proletariat was 'a government resting directly on violence and unrestrained by any rules or regulations'.[56]

The real responsibility for the current devastation of Russia Kozhinov attributes to those who in the twenties and early thirties stood for 'a complete break with the past' (*velikaya lomka*). By this (though he produces a few quotations to show that Lenin urged restraint) he must

mean the leaders of the Communist Party. And to forestall the accusa-
tion of targeting only the Jewish members of the Communist leadership,
he explicitly concentrates his attack on Bukharin, recently rehabilitated
and now much officially praised for having set forth an alternative model
of socialist construction in the late twenties, which might have enabled
the Soviet Union to continue the mixed economy of the twenties and
avoid the violent upheavals of the Stalinist model. Not at all, asserts
Kozhinov: Bukharin was an ally of Stalin on almost every point, and
different from him only on minor tactical questions. Kozhinov's argument is in fact an implied rejection of the October revolution and a plea
for a return to pre-revolutionary traditions; significantly, all he can find
to say in favour of the October revolution is that it *happened* and that
there is no point in discussing alternatives to it.[57]

What the Russian nationalists propose is an alternative model of
economic development designed to avoid the twin dangers of the
command economy and unregulated capitalism. This is the tradition of
what the critic Mikhail Antonov calls the 'civilised co-operative', by
which he means a modernised version of the peasant land commune
and the *artel'*, which I described in Chapter 2. Antonov criticises the
principal reform economists, such as Aganbegyan, Zaslavskaya and
Shmelyov, for remaining bogged down in the long-discredited economic categories of bourgeois society, for treating economics as a 'science
of production relations, which ignores the human being and the whole
moral and spiritual sphere of social life.' His own proposals are close in
spirit to the ideas of Schumacher or the West German Greens.

How far the newly grown Soviet co-operative movement can or will
evolve in this direction remains to be seen. But one of the pre-conditions
of its doing so is a much less rigidly regulated economic environment:
Antonov, in spite of his attacks on Stalin, inconsistently hankers after
official maintenance of the 'just price' and other features of the indigent
egalitarianism which the command economy imposed on the Soviet
peoples.[58] The danger is that in order to restrain the operation of the
market, especially as it may develop in the non-Russian republics, the
protagonists of the 'civilised co-operatives' will throw themselves into

the arms of an already hypertrophied party-state apparatus. The danger is aggravated by the Russian nationalists' habit of attributing the root of all evil – whether of the capitalist or Communist variety – to the Jews, for this renders them susceptible to the anti-Semitism and great power chauvinism of the late Stalin years, a combination which made possible the very administrative distortions they deplore. From that point of view, the failure of a reputable writer like Valentin Rasputin to distance himself from Pamyat' is a political mistake of major proportions.

The trouble is, Russian nationalism is not equivalent to the other nationalisms of the Soviet Union. Russians often ask me, 'Why shouldn't we be entitled to our own patriotism, like any other nation?' The answer is that Russia is so large and so dominant that Russian patriotism as a political force would unbalance the whole structure of the Soviet Union: it would split the Communist Party into its national components, something which is already beginning to happen, as we've seen, in the Caucasus and the Baltic. So an alliance between the 'revivalists' and the National Bolsheviks is in the best interests neither of the Communist Party nor of Russian patriots.

The fact is, and Soviet leaders must face it squarely, that the national question could break the Soviet Union. After all, it has broken all the other empires of the twentieth century, so why should the Soviet Union be an exception?

Actually, I think the strength of the armed forces and the security police gives it quite a good chance of being an exception for the foreseeable future. But all the same, if the Soviet leaders do not handle national aspirations with exemplary tact, then the only way they will be able to hold the whole explosive mixture together is by harnessing xenophobic Russian nationalism and by combining super-Brezhnevian corruption with military and police coercion on a scale which would distract the Soviet Union from its strategic commitments. That would be expensive, demoralising and internationally enfeebling.

The alternative is to convert the Soviet Union into a genuine federation. That is what it already is on paper, so it would only be necessary to breathe authentic life into institutions which already exist in suspended animation. I say 'only', but of course the task will be fraught with difficulty, especially since it will entail federalising the Communist Party, restoring meaning to the word 'democratic' in the formula of 'democratic centralism' which Lenin devised to describe its structure. Otherwise the national republics will never be able genuinely to determine their own economic, educational, social and other policies.

However, Gorbachev is already moving in this direction, democratising local party organisations and reforming the soviets so that they can fulfil real governmental functions. Nor would he actually be risking very much in conceding greater powers to the national republics: the armed forces and the KGB remain, as I say, quite strong enough in a territorially unified commonwealth to cope with most conceivable conflicts. And conflicts there would certainly be, as the example of Yugoslavia suggests. But federalisation would also bring great opportunities, and a release of creative energies which could enhance the wealth, strength and international standing of the Soviet Union. It is crucial that Russian patriots see this too, since, while other nations are oppressed in their name, they themselves will not be free.

6

Religion and
the atheist state

As I was leaving Tbilisi at the end of April 1988 I witnessed from the taxi an extraordinary event. On the Mekheti Church, high up on the crags which overlook the River Kura, two men were clambering over the roof, using an arrangement of ropes and pulleys to haul a golden cross on to the pinnacle. Inside, a service of dedication was being held: a church which had not seen divine worship for nearly seventy years was being returned to the faithful.

The day before in Moscow, Gorbachev had received Patriarch Pimen and five senior bishops. 'Believers', he told them, 'are Soviet working people and patriots, and they have every right to express their convictions in a fitting manner.'[1] This uncharacteristic statement was just the prelude to a series of festive occasions by which the leaders of state and church celebrated a millennium of Christianity. One of the high points was the restoration to the church of the Kiev Monastery of the Caves, on the site where the first baptism of the Russian peoples was reputed to have taken place a thousand years before.

It is not just the happy chance of the calendar which has brought church and state together. Many of the social problems Gorbachev is tackling today – corruption, alcoholism, slovenly work discipline, unstable family life – are moral rather than political in character. They have not responded to repeated campaigns of ideological exhortation mounted by the party's zealots. The party seems to have decided, doubtless reluctantly, that it might as well enlist the help of the established churches. Many of the country's best writers have been saying for years, even in the teeth of the censorship, that faith was an antidote to demoralisation. In any case, why alienate millions of believers – perhaps a third of the population – who would mostly be loyal and patriotic citizens were it not for the party's ingrained disdain for them?

The party, in short, is looking to the churches as a source of social solidarity which by itself it is poorly equipped to inspire. The Orthodox Church, which has long regarded *sobornost'* – the spirit of community – as its distinctive strength, ought to be ideally fitted to supply this deficiency.

Today, however, one can no longer be confident of its ability to do so. The trouble is that the church has been seriously, perhaps fatally, weakened by the party's own past treatment of it. Decades of active persecution alternating with contemptuous manipulation have left it not only numerically reduced but spiritually debilitated to the extent where it may no longer be able to play the role the party now envisages for it.

The heritage of bad, at times murderous, church–state relations is a grievous one. From the very beginning the Soviet state expropriated the church, and declared the clergy more or less outcasts. The Law on Religious Associations limited religious worship strictly to designated churches and prayer houses. It forbade Sunday schools or any form of religious instruction, pastoral visits, or charitable work. In other words, the state tacitly outlawed any religious activity other than the performance of divine service. Normal parish life was rendered impossible, and religion became, as one might say, a matter for consenting adults in private. Those provisions have remained in force to the present day.

The Orthodox Church eventually accepted this situation, though not without damaging internal rifts. In 1927 Metropolitan Sergii, locum tenens for the vacant Patriarchate, proclaimed, 'We wish to be Orthodox believers, and at the same time to acknowledge the Soviet Union as our civil motherland, whose joys and successes are our joys and successes, and whose misfortunes are our misfortunes.' Asked privately how he could accept such a humiliating predicament, he replied, 'We must preserve the Church for the people; after that, the Lord will show us what we must do.'[2] Survival at any price has become paramount in the Russian Orthodox Church. This caution derives not just from difficult relations with the state, but also from the uncertain allegiance of the people. Russia's élites and intellectuals have a long history of heresy and unbelief. As for ordinary people, the Church was worried long before the revolution that they would fall prey to the numerous non-conformist sects, or indeed to the other religions which perforce coexisted in the multi-national Russian Empire: Catholicism, Lutheranism, Judaism, Islam. Against this background, and with the added threat of the militantly atheist Communist Party, simply keeping the Church in being was a daunting challenge, and doubtless it was in that spirit that Sergii made his gesture of reconciliation.

Unfortunately, though, Sergii's declaration of loyalty to the Soviet state induced no reciprocal concessions. The 1930s were the grimmest period the churches – and not just the Orthodox Church – had ever experienced. The collectivisation of agriculture often meant the closure of the village church, and sometimes its physical destruction, though more usually it would be turned into a storehouse or club room. Priests were arrested and sent to labour camps or driven into exile along with the 'kulaks'. Of more than 50,000 churches open before the revolution, only some 4,000 remained by 1939. Of 163 bishops, only four were still at liberty.[3]

At that juncture, in spite of all its concessions to a brazen atheist state, the very survival of the Orthodox Church was in doubt. Yet Stalin never completed its destruction. In 1939, when the Soviet Union annexed what had formerly been Eastern Poland, he decided that the Church could help to assimilate the region's largely Ukrainian and Belorussian population. During the war, he was glad to co-opt the Church as an ally in the patriotic struggle, and encouraged the faithful to raise the money for a tank column named after the medieval prince Dmitrii Donskoi. In 1943, when he was beginning to envisage taking control of Eastern Europe, Stalin received Metropolitan Sergii in audience (the only such occasion in Soviet history till Gorbachev repeated it in 1988) and he allowed the Church to re-establish an ecclesiastical administration, to publish a journal, to reopen some of its parishes and to resume training recruits for the priesthood. Thereafter – and right up to the present – the Orthodox Church has been a useful ally of the Soviet state in its diplomatic relations throughout the world, and especially in the international peace movement.

At a certain stage, then, the Soviet leaders decided that the Church would be more useful to them alive than dead, or perhaps one should say open than clandestine. That was a fateful decision, and maybe in a sense it justified Sergii's act of submission. In spite of renewed persecution by Khrushchev in the sixties, under which at least half the existing parishes were closed down, the Church *has* survived as a recognisable entity to the present more favourable juncture, when the Soviet intelligentsia is displaying renewed interest in religion and the state seems inclined to make concessions.

On the other hand that survival has been secured at a very high price. Enfeebled by subservience to an atheist state, the Church is no longer well fitted to act as vehicle for the religious revival or to promote social solidarity. New converts feel acutely the absence of any normal parish life. As a lay Soviet believer commented a few years ago, 'In the Church there is almost no Christian interpersonal sociability, no activity in fulfilment of the second commandment. How many lonely old people are too weak to leave their homes for bread or medicine, but the people with whom they have prayed together for years don't even know of their plight.'[4] If this is so, then the Church is not fulfilling the very ideal of *sobornost'* – the spirit of congregation – which it used to claim as its distinctive strength.

Besides, the system of ecclesiastical appointment ensures that priests and bishops are chosen, as far as possible, for their deference to the party. Patronage is ultimately in the hands of the Communist Party Central Committee, like all other serious personnel questions in the Soviet Union. It is delegated through a state committee called the Council for Religious Affairs, which reports regularly on the comportment of every priest and bishop. A few years ago the text of one of these confidential reports reached the west. It divided bishops into three categories, according to the degree of their compliance with party policy. The first, most favoured category, consists of those who 'realistically understand that our state is not interested in proclaiming the role of . . . the Church in society and accordingly do not display any particular zeal in extending the influence of Orthodoxy among the population'. Less favoured is a second category: those bishops who correctly observe the law on cults, but nevertheless 'stand for the heightening of the role of the Church in personal, family and public life', who 'select for priestly office . . . zealous adherents of Orthodox piety'. Third and last, the Council deplores those bishops who 'have made attempts to evade the law on cults' and who slander the Council's commissioners, 'falsifying the position in their dioceses'.[5] Presumably they have been doing something like sanctioning unauthorised Sunday schools and then misleading official informers.

This report prompts mixed reflections. On the one hand, any appointments system adopting these criteria is likely to produce a submissive church hierarchy. On the other hand, I am intrigued by the intermediate category – the largest numerically. It suggests a substantial contingent of bishops who, under the mask of outward conformity, are discreetly doing what they can to extend the Church's influence and to prepare for its future. One is reminded that, even in the most abject times, the Orthodox Church has remained a source of spiritual strength for many, partly through its liturgy, partly through the ascetic, contemplative tradition of its elders and holy men, whose effect on believers derived not least from the fact that they had no institutional place in the church, but acted by virtue of their personal charisma. Father Zosima in Dostoevskii's *The Brothers Karamazov* was based on a real-life model of this kind. Today the monastic heritage has been almost completely destroyed, but there is still fitful evidence that a few such holy men have helped to keep alive the faith through the recent bleak decades.[6]

Because of its enserfed position, the Russian Orthodox Church has had little opportunity to adjust to the huge social changes of the twentieth century. It remains essentially the same Church which used to tend an overwhelmingly peasant congregation. Now the faith of peasants was very different from that of the contemporary urban intellectual. The Russian peasant's religion was a largely illiterate one – a rustic faith based on the liturgy and icons. It followed the rhythms of the agricultural cycle, and it was interwoven with a rich overlay of pagan elements, especially those associated with the peasant hut and the ancestors.[7]

In the early twentieth century ecclesiastical reformers did try to modernise the liturgy, improve religious education, encourage a livelier parish life and break down the social divisions within the church. But the tsarist regime resisted them and then – even more lethal – the Bolshevik one favoured them, laying reformers open to the charge of serving as the agents of atheism in splitting and undermining the church from within. Today's Orthodox Church has not forgotten the experience and has drawn from it the lesson that reform is divisive and therefore mortally dangerous to a church under siege.

Today, however, the old peasant faith is more or less dead – its passing mourned in Valentin Rasputin's magnificent novel, *Farewell to Matyora*, published in 1976.[8] The educated young people of the modern city are seeking something very different: a highly literate faith, based on a knowledge of the Bible and the church fathers, of ecclesiastical history and theology, a faith capable of holding its own in the intellectual contest with Marxism and other secular philosophies. Soviet intellectuals are, I think, peculiarly prone to the religious urge. After all, they have been brought up to an ideology which demanded submergence of the ego in the collective for the sake of an exalted aim, the building of an earthly paradise. Not only have they thoroughly imbibed the catechisms of that doctrine, but they have participated in public rituals designed to consolidate it, and they have made their obeisances to its icons. Communism has never been a religion in the full sense of the word, but it has adopted many of the outward appurtenances of one. When its conviction fades, therefore, as it certainly has in the Soviet Union, it is natural that many of its adherents should seek a genuine religion to put in its place.

They come, moreover, from a faith whose teachings are expounded in a comprehensive and reasoned manner. They will expect a church to present its doctrines no less convincingly. This is where the Russian Orthodox Church often fails to live up to their expectations.

Some have dealt with this vacuum in their own way, by setting up study groups and seminars, putting together small libraries of religious works, which are otherwise so difficult to obtain in the Soviet Union. They hold regular meetings to exchange ideas or even simple information. This is the *kruzhok* again – the cohesive little circle which is the natural habitat of the Russian intelligentsia – and it not only fills the intellectual deficiency, but also compensates for the absence of a proper congregational life within the Church. One such *kruzhok* was established in Moscow in 1974 by a cinema student, Aleksandr Ogorodnikov. He brought together friends who had grown up in atheist families and then gone through a complex, sometimes agonising process of spiritual questing. 'From Marxist convictions, via nihilism and the complete rejection of any ideology,' Ogorodnikov later recalled, 'via attraction to the "hippy" lifestyle, we came to the Church.' Even there, they found no secure haven, partly because of what they called their 'pagan intellectual pride', but partly because of the 'lack of a flourishing community life within the Orthodox Church'. As Ogorodnikov said: 'Our thirst for spiritual communion, religious education and missionary service runs up against all the might of the state's repressive machinery.'

The seminar met irregularly, with a fluctuating membership whose only qualification was readiness to join in what under Soviet conditions was a hazardous enterprise, but it recreated for some of its members the *sobornost'* – that spirit of community – which they felt they had not found in the Church itself. 'We loved that little flat', one of its members has testified, 'for the spirit of freedom which filled it . . . Those conversations, that way of life, took hold of me completely: it was all . . . so full of meaning and depth, so full of the warmth and genuine feeling which you cannot confuse with anything else; it was so different from vulgar Soviet life . . .'[9]

Well, 'vulgar Soviet life' supervened. Members of the seminar were searched, interrogated and harassed. Ogorodnikov was deprived of his residence permit for Moscow, then arrested for 'parasitism' and sent to a labour camp. Other members were charged with disseminating the journal, *Obshchina* (*Community*), which they had started to bring out. The Soviet state in the late seventies was not prepared to tolerate this kind of religious seeking.[10]

The church hierarchy is vulnerable to the charge that it did not do enough to intercede for young people like these endeavouring to take up a Christian way of life. When I asked Metropolitan Filaret, a senior bishop, about them a few years ago, he replied that, since they had never entered the Church, he could do nothing for them. Besides, he added, they criticise irresponsibly, bringing conflict and disharmony into our church and sowing hatred where there should be love. The leaders of state and party are our flock, and for the sake of the Russian people as a whole we should approach them in a spirit of dialogue, not one of rejection.[11]

Fair enough, if the state had not taken the lead in sowing the disharmony. But Filaret's attitude also reveals a very understandable aspiration: the desire to play once again a full role in society, to be part of the Russian people, coexisting in dialogue with a ruling party which has a very different philosophy. If church legislation currently being discussed is passed, this may again be possible. Published drafts envisage religious organisations resuming the status of juridical persons, including that of owning property, receiving the right to conduct religious education in church and home, and to conduct public ceremonies. Church bells, silent for decades, would be allowed to peal again. Priests would be allowed to visit the sick and take confessions in hospital. On the other hand, congregations would still be required to register with the authorities before being recognised as legitimate religious organisations, a stipulation which in the past has provided a lever for political interference.[12]

The man in charge of the Church's side of the legislative drafting process, Archbishop Kirill of Smolensk, gave a lecture in London in July 1988. In it he acknowledged that the Church had not been able to play its proper role in Soviet society. Much of the task of transmitting the Christian spirituality of the past had, he pointed out, been accomplished by *writers*, even by writers who were not themselves believers, but who derived their inspiration from Russia's cultural heritage. Now, he said, the priority of 'all-human values' – non-political values, in other words – was at last recognised once again by the political leadership, and therewith the Church faced the opportunity and the challenge of resuming its proper role. Whether it would respond successfully to this challenge he left an open question. And so would I. It remains to be seen whether enough of the Church's underlying spiritual strength has survived to enable it to meet the needs of its potential flock today.

If the Orthodox Church is not in a fit condition to receive the questing young people of today, then it has a formidable rival among Christian denominations. The fastest growing church in the Soviet period has been the Union of Evangelical Christians and Baptists, formed during the war under state supervision to bring together a variety of Protestant denominations.

The reason for its relative success is partly that, like the non-conformist chapels of Victorian Britain, it has filled the gaps left by the official Church in the cheerless new industrial towns. Where the Orthodox Church has been forbidden to build, the more informal congregations of the Baptists have inconspicuously taken root, using temporary prayer houses, or even each other's apartments. Their presbyters are mostly unpaid, with full-time jobs in the secular world, and they devote their spare time to pastoral work. They are overworked but flexible, able to adapt readily to Soviet life.

Perhaps most important of all, the Baptists offer a warm and supportive community, which, by all reports, rallies round its own needy members, helping the old and sick, giving relief and sometimes financial aid to one-parent families. This may be why they were the first to practise a form of social solidarity later adopted by secular dissenters. In 1964 families of persecuted Baptists set up a Council of Prisoners' Relatives, to obtain data about co-believers imprisoned for their faith, to collect funds for their aid, and to write appeals to the authorities.[13]

In a sense the Baptists practise what the Communists preach. They live lives of hard work, sobriety, moderate asceticism and mutual aid; they are patriotic and law-abiding. They have inherited the best qualities of the old peasant community. Yet with all that theirs is a religion of the literate, in which sermons and the study of the scriptures occupy a paramount place, and it is natural that it should attract so many people in a society which has been moving fast towards universal literacy.

All the same, some elements of their faith are in direct tension with the atheist state. Close study of the scriptures is difficult to keep up when the authorities permit very few Bibles to be printed. The Baptist ideal of the autonomy of each congregation and the separation of church and state is incompatible with strict official supervision of the churches. Above all, the duty to evangelise, to bring up children in the faith and to convert unbelievers, runs directly counter to the party's religious policy.

Disagreement over how to react to this incompatibility split the Baptists in the sixties. Whereas the leadership of the Baptist Union took the line that they must preach the gospel only within permitted limits, some congregations denounced this policy as 'rendering unto Caesar that which is God's', and insisted on their right and duty to bring children to services, and to seek converts in the world.[14] These non-conformists, calling themselves Initsiativniki or reform Baptists, suffered heavily from persecution during the Khrushchev and Brezhnev periods. In 1966 they managed to organise the first unofficial public demonstration to be seen in the Soviet Union for forty years, when 500 delegates came from 130 cities to present a petition to Brezhnev. Not being received, they sat in the courtyard of the Supreme Soviet's Presidium, and eventually had to be bodily carried away, singing hymns, by the police.[15]

So the Baptists have been a major force. They do not on the whole attract intellectuals, for their theology is unsophisticated, but they have done much to provide for the religious aspirations of workers and employees, especially perhaps those recently uprooted from a traditional rural way of life. With perhaps a million and a half members,[16] they are not all that numerous, but they are still growing, and they have been political innovators, offering an example of solidarity under pressure from which others have learnt. Their conflicts with the authorities show how a religious movement with an effective community spirit can make life difficult for an unreconstructed atheist state. If the Orthodox Church disappoints the party's hopes through insufficient *sobornost'*, the Baptists may prove to have an excess of it.

Although Islam springs from a very different origin, it does in some ways resemble the Evangelical faith: it is fiercely committed and egalitarian, but also flexible, able to accommodate itself to Soviet life. In the early years of the Soviet regime Islam and communism had much in common: a commitment to equality, the brotherhood of nations and the struggle against western imperialism. But the temporary alliance between them soon split apart: the atheism of Moscow fitted ill with the fervent theism of Islam, and Asiatic ties pulled Muslims away from the orbit of European Russia.

We know relatively little about Islam in the Soviet Union today. Few Sovietologists command the necessary languages, and we receive scant information from the relevant geographical areas. Except among the Crimean Tartars, there appears to be little or no dissent as we understand that term. What evidence we have suggests that Muslims quietly distance themselves from the Soviet mainstream, discreetly maintaining their traditional way of life in its essentials, while conceding inessentials to secular society. People stay in villages and small towns, with their social round centred on the tea-house, their religious life on the mosque or Sufi brotherhood, rather than move into the large cities with their more anonymous lifestyle. One consequence of this tendency is that the birth rate remains much higher than in the European parts of the Soviet Union. Large families, encouraged by both religion and custom, are the norm, and the Muslim peoples, already at least a sixth of the Soviet population, are steadily increasing their share. But they are too attached to their homeland to move to European Russia or Siberia to fill the labour shortages there.

Soviet Muslims are reluctant, then, to leave their small towns and villages. They accept what socialist society has to offer them: broader education, relative prosperity and greater freedom for women, while at the same time they adapt their religious practices to the work patterns imposed by the planned economy. There is not in any case the sharp distinction between the sacred and the secular in Islam that we are used to in Christianity. To say 'I am a Muslim' is more to acknowledge membership of a specific community or to deny being European than it is to assert a conscious confessional choice. In other words, it may be an ethnic as much as a religious statement. This means that custom and worship can mingle in a relatively relaxed manner. If a month's fasting at Ramadan is too demanding for a Soviet production worker who must keep up his bodily strength, then it can legitimately be curtailed to as little as three days. Or the requirement to pray five times a day prostrated in the direction of Mecca can be modified to once or twice in a posture more suited to the layout of office or factory floor. In general, the customs which have survived best are those connected with family and community life, such as circumcision, marriage and burial, rather than with religion *per se.*[17]

It is important to remember, though, that beyond official Islam, sanctioned by the Soviet state, lies the forbidden milieu of the Sufi brotherhoods. Descendants of the holy orders which headed the resistance to Russian colonisation in the nineteenth century, they preserve the Islamic faith in its purest, most uncompromising form. By their very nature we know little about the brotherhoods, but it seems certain that they are abiding sources of unofficial education, spiritual guidance and cultural transmission in a society torn between the sacred and the secular.[18]

Some scholars would maintain that a Muslim explosion of some kind is imminent. It is true there *have* been isolated outbursts in recent years, but not quite the sustained unrest one might have expected following the Iranian revolution and the Soviet invasion of Afghanistan.[19] What little evidence we have seems to me to suggest a pliant and flexible but self-respecting network of ethnic communities unostentatiously preserving and extending what they can of their heritage. This quiet build-up could lead to serious trouble one day, but all we are justified in diagnosing at the moment is a gradual and persistent reassertion of traditional cultural and religious patterns.

Altogether, what we see in the manifold religious denominations of the Soviet Union is a discreet but determined revival of inherited faiths and traditional community life, altered but not rendered unrecognisable by the pressures of modern society. The party welcomes the strengthening of social solidarity, but it may find the accompanying ideological outlook hard to swallow. Some of the churches which have best sustained their community spirit are the national ones, in Georgia, Armenia and Lithuania, for example. Their ethnic aspirations, though peacefully expressed, could intensify the conflict between nationalities which is already such a headache for the authorities.

The most remarkable case of this kind is the Ukrainian Catholic Church, which Stalin forcibly merged with the Russian Orthodox Church at an illegally convened synod in 1946. Some of its followers became more or less reluctant communicants of the Russian Church, but many refused to surrender their separate identity and attached themselves to unregistered priests or itinerant monks. In the intervening decades, the Church has flourished underground because it offers Ukrainians a way of celebrating their faith in their own language, and of marking their alienation from a Russian-dominated atheist system.[20]

The election of Pope John Paul II, who explicitly supported the Ukrainian Catholics, brought renewed hope of legalisation, and 1982 saw the appearance of an Initiative Group for the Defence of the Rights of Believers of the Church in Ukraine, which began to bring out a journal to publicise violations of freedom of conscience and worship. Its leading members were soon imprisoned or driven into exile. Popular support for the Church was further intensified by the appearance of the Virgin Mary to a twelve-year-old peasant girl in the village of Hrushevo on the first anniversary of the Chernobyl' explosion in April 1987. Pilgrimages and processions followed, in which other believers claimed to have had visions of the Virgin Mary telling them the Ukrainians were a 'chosen people' and should break free of the Soviet yoke.[21]

The state's *rapprochement* with other denominations has not yet brought any improvement in the status of the Ukrainian Catholic Church. Many Ukrainians suspect that the main obstacle is not so much the Soviet state as the Russian Orthodox Church, which stands to lose millions of believers in a region where, for historical reasons, its parishes are especially numerous.

Altogether, seeking an alliance with the churches is a promising but high-risk policy. The Soviet Union is already a much more 'religious' country than Britain or most of Western Europe, not least because of the utopian aspirations embedded in its official ideology. On top of this, the current religious revival has all the elemental force of the 'return of the repressed'. The party's new allies may restore a lost sense of community and improve the morale of Soviet society, but they are likely also to intensify its suppressed divisions. The churches bid fair, moreover, to rival the party on its own ground of socialisation and ideological indoctrination. All this will enliven Soviet politics and make it more honest, but it may give the party a bumpy ride. As a Russian proverb says: 'Two bears don't get on well in the same den.'

7

The paradox of
Gorbachev's reforms

In the foregoing chapters I have been making my case for the assertion that civil society is re-emerging, in very diverse forms, from under the totalitarian carapace, and is beginning to make itself felt in the political system hitherto monopolised by the Communist Party. Having thus, as it were, put the cart before the horse, I'd like to end where most observers would begin, and examine how the political leadership sees the situation and what changes it would like to bring about.

That means looking closely at Mr Gorbachev. He has established such a position of dominance, and stamped his personal style so markedly on the current reform programme, that one is bound to ask how such a man could appear in the midst of what we are used to regarding as the faceless Communist Party apparatus.

One manifest difference between Gorbachev and his predecessors is that he is younger and much better educated. That is, he is more representative of the urban and sophisticated society that the Soviet Union is becoming. But that alone is not to say much. It is the *kind* of education and early experience which is crucial. Gorbachev comes from the fertile southern region of Stavropol', an area of Cossack traditions and rich peasant farming, which underwent severe famine after collectivisation in the first year or two of the young Mikhail's life. When he became party first secretary in Stavropol' nearly forty years later, he devoted a lot of attention to agriculture, which, as elsewhere in the country, was in a grossly demoralised state. He even took a correspondence course in agricultural economics. His studies as well as his direct observations led him to promote an experiment for motivating collective farmers which was currently out of favour in Moscow: the farm labour force was divided into brigades of 15 to 30 people, each of them was assigned a fixed area of land, together with seeds and equipment, and was then paid according to the results achieved. Under this regime, wheat output rose 30–50 per cent over a few years, and Gorbachev was permitted to continue the practice, even though many *apparatchiks* worried that the brigade system meant the beginning of the break-up of the collective farms and a reversion to private agriculture.[1]

The other major component of Gorbachev's formative experience was his law course at Moscow University in the early fifties. In the west, to say that a budding politician studied law sounds unremarkable. Most Soviet politicians, by contrast, start their careers with technological studies rounded off by a course at a Higher Party School. Law has been looked down upon as faintly 'bourgeois'. Gorbachev, then, set out in a distinctive way. Now jurisprudence in Stalin's time was far from liberal in spirit, but all the same he will have had to familiarise himself with Roman law and western constitutional law, and it is fair to suppose that this may have given him the makings of a rather different outlook on the problems of Soviet society from that held by his colleagues. This was important to a leader who was to come to power at a time when social groups with their own distinct interests and aspirations were beginning to assert themselves and to interact; for if there was to be peaceful mediation between them, then it could only be through the processes of the law.

At the same time Gorbachev was secretary of the Komsomol in his faculty, and subsequently spent nearly thirty years in the party apparatus – sufficient, one might suppose, to obliterate any trace of nostalgia for what he had learned in law school. He achieved the highest office in 1985 as the candidate of those who wanted change, or at least realised it could no longer be postponed. His mentor was Brezhnev's immediate successor, Andropov, also an intelligent and by all accounts uncorrupt figure determined to bring about change, but so moulded by fifteen years of heading the security police that his thoughts turned naturally to discipline and the eradication of corruption as the principal instrument of regeneration. It is true that he was open to the possibility that some decentralisation of the economy was required, but he was already too old and ill on attaining office to undertake any serious steps in this direction.

This was Gorbachev's immediate inheritance. He became General Secretary of the party in March 1985 with the support of the KGB, among others, and for his first year or so in office he could be plausibly seen as Andropov's disciple. He tightened labour discipline, invoking the legendary feats of the Donbass coalminer Alexei Stakhanov; he established an official quality control inspectorate, Gospriyomka, which was instructed to reject shoddy manufactured goods and dock the pay of those responsible; he continued and even stepped up the dismissal and criminal investigation of corrupt officials; notoriously, he sharply restricted the sale of vodka and banned its use in official institutions, even for celebrations. Henceforth mineral water had to be substituted, an affront to Russian traditions of sociability and hospitality which earned Gorbachev the none too affectionate nickname of 'Mineral Secretary'.

This, if you like, was perestroika Mark 1, the fruit of Gorbachev's long experience in the apparatus. It was launched with a new and lively style of presentation, television interviews, question-and-answer sessions with workers on the shopfloor, during which Gorbachev *talked* about technological innovation, about greater openness or glasnost, about encouraging personal initiative in the economy, but made very little progress towards these goals.

Then, some time in the summer or autumn of 1986 there was a real change, partly in words but even more in substance. Perhaps this was a transition to a more radical transformation which Gorbachev had long intended to carry out; more likely it was the result of learning on the job just how deep the crisis was, and therefore how far-reaching were the measures needed to grapple with it. The explosion at the Chernobyl' nuclear power station in April 1986 certainly dramatised the defects of the system, revealing as it did the mortal dangers of handling awesome technological power with such secretive and slovenly irresponsibility.

The aftermath of Chernobyl' underlined the shortcomings of restricted glasnost in creating hostility abroad and panic at home. Foreigners were indignant at Soviet obfuscation in a matter affecting public health all round the world. As for Soviet citizens, thousands of them were besieging the railway stations to flee from unknown dangers they could only learn about from foreign broadcasts. Chernobyl' might have been calculated to reawaken Gorbachev's interest in the legal studies of his youth; and he had many advisers on hand to tell him that freedom of speech and the rule of law were prerequisites for any lasting improvement in society. In December 1986 he released from exile one of the earliest protagonists of this doctrine, Academician Andrei Sakharov.

This was the onset of Gorbachev's perestroika Mark 2, which soon led him into uncharted territories, awakening suspicion and resentment among some of those who had helped him to come to power. Above all it alarmed the medium and lower level party-state officials, those sufficiently well placed to enjoy a modicum of power, privilege and the 'emoluments of office' under the existing system, but not high enough to realise or perhaps care about the depth of the crisis. Gorbachev was strengthening the supervision of these *apparatchiks* by affecting it from below as well as from above: that is by encouraging ordinary workers to report on the shortcomings and transgressions of their managers, their trade union officials and party secretaries. Stalin had of course encouraged this too back in the thirties, but his chosen vehicle, the anonymous denunciation – the infamous *donos* which sent so many innocent men and women to their deaths – was utterly discredited. Instead of the *donos* Gorbachev proposed increased openness and democracy: public meetings, letters (signed) to the press, and the election of responsible officials by their subordinates.

An intriguing theme began to make an occasional appearance in his speeches at this time: that is that the absence of an opposition party obliged party officials to be especially searching in their self-criticism, and to respond with alacrity and probity to criticism from others. In a televised speech at Khabarovsk he warned that 'officials who react to criticism by persecuting their critics lay themselves open to criminal prosecution'.[2] Significantly, these words, which were clearly heard on television, were omitted from the newspaper version of the speech, for they enunciated a novel and unwelcome principle: that in certain circumstances the law ranks higher than party hierarchies. This is where the perestroika Mark 1 practice of cleaning up corruption began to intersect with the Mark 2 theory of the rule of law. Gorbachev was beginning to see how a legal system with real teeth could strengthen Soviet society.

He was talking now, furthermore, not just of 'restructuring', but of a transformation of social consciousness, of a 'revolution . . . in the hearts and minds of the people'.[3] This implied opening up the whole field of culture and education. If he was going to take on the party-state apparatus, then he needed an alliance with the cultural and scientific intelligentsia, whose importance, as we have seen, is out of all proportion to their fast growing but still relatively limited numbers. In June 1986 he met a delegation of writers and appealed to them for help. The people want change, he declared, and the leadership wants change, but in between stands 'a managerial stratum, the ministerial and party apparatus, which does not . . . want to give up its . . . privileges'.[4]

The writers, despite divisions among themselves, responded to his appeal with their own brand of public spirit. Their congress spearheaded a public campaign against the diversion of the northern rivers, they called for the abolition of censorship and they turned some of their journals into bastions and exemplars of glasnost. Joined by a few campaigning newspapers editors, film directors and courageous historians, they published hitherto forbidden authors, and opened up Soviet history once more as a serious subject of study. Stalin's crimes were exposed as never before, even in Khrushchev's thaw: his vilification and hounding of the opposition, the brutal collectivisation of agriculture and the consequent famine, the arrests and executions, the deportations of whole peoples, the costly mistakes in wartime leadership – all these half-suppressed and wholly suppressed topics were exposed week after week to a public that seemed insatiable. People would come weeping out of a film like *Repentance*, which was a vivid allegorical representation of Stalin's repressions. Nothing could be more revealing about the profundity of the trauma the Soviet people have undergone than the stunned and fixed attention they accorded the revelation of fifty-year-old crimes. 'It's as if we can breathe again freely,' a friend said to me. Even many young people, not directly affected by Stalin, seemed to sense relief at this exorcising of his ghost.

On the other hand, this spirit of enquiry does not yet fully extend to Lenin or the October revolution. No more than timid, semi-veiled questions have been raised about the institutions which Stalin inherited from Lenin, even though writers like Soloukhin and Kozhinov have described graphically some of the results of their lawlessness even in the pre-Stalin period (see above, p. 108). This reticence presumably explains the decision not to publish any of the works of Alexander Solzhenitsyn, which are now wholly acceptable as regards their picture of Stalin, but which explicitly attribute a major share of the responsibility to Lenin for making his mass murders possible. [5]

Glasnost does not only touch on the past: it applies also to many aspects of the present. The media comment with much greater frankness and openness on the evils of today, which they present moreover not just as regrettable aberrations, but as failings of the system. The housing shortage, poor work discipline, shoddy consumer goods and lamentable medical care are expounded and analysed in vivid detail. Statistics are at last being published on alcoholism, suicide, disease and mortality. Crucial political decisions are widely and sometimes critically discussed. There are limits, especially in the treatment of foreign and military policy, and to some extent of the national problem: reporting from Armenia, for instance, has been restricted and anodyne, Soviet spokesmen arguing that restraint is necessary to avoid exacerbating an already turbulent situation. Nor has there been any full-scale debate about the aftermath of the Chernobyl' disaster, the prospects for rendering nuclear power generation safe, and the alternatives if that cannot be done. In general, though, the last two or three years have offered the Soviet public an unprecedented wealth of information and ideas on the state of their country. And the public has responded, queuing from early morning to buy journals and newspapers which have acquired a reputation for honesty and liveliness.[6]

Whatever the effervescence of debate in the political field, it is in the economy that the legacy of the past weighs most heavily and implacably. Traditional practices have corrupted producers and reduced consumers to a state of resentful but helpless apathy, so that serious change, if it happens at all, is bound to be prolonged and painful. The economic system established by Stalin has proved, despite all its conspicuous deficiencies, to be forbiddingly stable and self-reinforcing. As I pointed out in the first chapter, it provides for most of the population job tenure and a guaranteed minimum sufficiency of material provision in return for a low standard of living and absence of control over workplace decision-making. This is a bargain which the majority of the Soviet population has tacitly accepted and they are apprehensive of seeing it violated, for fear of the disruptions that might well follow.

In some ways, in fact, the Soviet state has perpetuated the attitudes of the pre-1930 Russian village community. The expectation is still prevalent that the community will guarantee essentials in a context of comradely indigence just above the poverty line. This shared privation generates natural fears about what economic reform might entail, as well as resentment of those who benefit from the new atmosphere to indulge in some newly legalised private enterprise. How many times over the last year or two have I heard Soviet citizens use the word 'speculator' to disparage private traders or co-operatives providing at high prices goods and services seldom available at all in the state sector?

This sullen egalitarianism dovetails neatly with the interest of the party-state apparatus in retaining their network of controls and hence their grip on the economy. It is also especially common in Russia, as distinct from the other nations of the Soviet empire, maybe because the village community was more cohesive and lasted longer there than elsewhere. However that may be, most observers would agree that private enterprise is likely to be both more successful and more socially acceptable in the Baltic or the Caucasus, even perhaps in Central Asia, than in Russia itself. Such ethnic discrepancies harbour considerable dangers, for they mean that effective economic reforms may intensify conflicts between the various Soviet nations, with their different levels of economic achievement and expectation. The damaging rivalries between the various republics of Yugoslavia are a warning; and in the Soviet Union the situation would be aggravated by the fact that the nation which may prove economically most backward is also the largest and most powerful.

This resistance, or at any rate, inertia, is reinforced by the practical difficulties of implementing reform. So many institutions and so many attitudes have to be changed that it cannot be done at one blow. For instance, it is virtually impossible in conditions of scarcity and imbalance simultaneously to abolish the system of centralised supply allocation (*Gossnab*), and also to carry out a comprehensive price reform, letting goods find their own level on the wholesale market. Nor is it easy for enterprise managers to break away from dependence on the state to find their own suppliers and customers, a task to which they are entirely unaccustomed, and for which in any case normal market information is largely lacking. Yet if these changes are not carried through, then enterprises cannot in any meaningful sense exercise the autonomy they have been granted by the law of July 1987. They continue to rely on the state for raw materials, spare parts and fuel, and their negotiations with potential customers are still distorted by administratively determined prices which may bear no relation to supply and demand. One has to agree with the British economist Alec Nove that 'To change everything at once is impossible, but partial change creates contradictions and inconsistencies.'[7]

The inherent difficulties of reform are further aggravated by the inconsistencies of the leadership. Perestroika Mark 1 persists and interferes with perestroika Mark 2. When Gorbachev came to power, he began by continuing Andropov's policy of trying to reinvigorate the economy by tightening up and disciplining the existing system. He proclaimed the need for technological innovation and 'acceleration' (*uskorenie*). He established Gospriyomka. He cracked down on alcohol consumption. He shut down some of the old ministries and set up super new state agencies to run whole branches of the economy, like machine building, energy and agriculture. He imposed new penalties for receiving 'non-labour income', to try and restrict the black economy.[8]

It is true that from the outset Gorbachev also proclaimed his intention to decentralise the economy by offering individual enterprises more autonomy. But by the time the new enterprise law came into effect, on 1 January 1988, the new institutions of centralisation and discipline were already thoroughly in the saddle, their strength bolstered by decades of custom and self-interest. Not surprisingly, then, enterprise required to cope with 'self-financing' found it simplest to continue fulfilling imposed production targets, now renamed 'state contract orders' (goszakazy), which account for all or nearly all of their output. As the economist V. Selyunin says: 'Either you can have uskorenie, or you can have perestroika. You cannot have both.'[9]

In this way too, increasing aggregate growth has the paradoxical effect of exacerbating shortages, since it enfeebles enterprise autonomy and thwarts the working of the market. It does not even result in more goods that people can use. In the words of Premier Ryzhkov: 'We produce more tractors in this country than all the capitalist countries put together. And yet we don't have enough tractors.'[10] Or as the reform economist Otto Latsis puts it: 'They build irrigation channels which bring no increase in agricultural production. They produce machine tools for which there are no operators, tractors for which there are no drivers, and threshing machines which they know will not work. Further millions of people supply these superfluous products with electricity, ore, oil and coal. In return they receive their wages like everyone else, and take them to the shops. There, however, they find no goods to buy, because their work has not produced any.'[11] So the economy grows, and the shortages grow with it.

Agriculture is a special problem. The villages have never recovered from the demoralisation of the brutal and humiliating collectivisation imposed by Stalin. Whatever experiments Gorbachev may have tried in Stavropol', since coming to power he has been hesitant about tampering with the collective and state farms as the keystone of the system of

agricultural production and delivery. Indeed he strengthened the existing system in some ways by the creation of a new super-ministry for
agriculture and food-processing, Gosagroprom. This characteristic
brainchild of perestroika Mark 1 soon established its deadening grip, and
by 1989, according to *Pravda*, was 'flooding the collective farms with
instructions and regulations,' while its offices churned out more than
five thousand categories of forms and bulletins, containing eight million
planning indicators. [12]

Unabashed, Gorbachev soon began to move smartly in the opposite
direction, towards the principle that 'small is beautiful', by encouraging
the creation of contract brigades from units as small as the individual
household or family. [13] He went on from there to urge collective farm
chairmen to offer such miniature 'brigades' long-term leases of land, up
to fifty years at a time. This campaign was accompanied by the
rehabilitation of Bukharin, who in the twenties had argued for a gradual
'co-operatisation' of farms as an alternative to full-scale collectivisation.
These moves seemed to presage a transition to an essentially private
agriculture, with former collective and state farms acting as co-
operatives to provide bulk purchasing, agrarian expertise and marketing
services. [14]

Gorbachev has hesitated, however, to take the final step, presumably
because of fears in the rural party apparatus of losing their authority and
indeed the lion's share of their current function. At the long-awaited
Central Committee plenum on agriculture in March 1989, Gorbachev
abolished Gosagroprom, but reaffirmed that the collective principle
would stay and that there was no intention to return to private property
in land. Otherwise he merely reiterated his commitment to changes
already announced, that is to a mixture of collective and private
leasehold farming. [15]

These changes have not generated a marked increase in food production, and they are unlikely to. Land is available to be leased, but both the
collective farms, as its current owners, and the peasants, the potential
lessees of it, are proving reluctant to take up the opportunity. Some
commentators attribute this reluctance to the 'depeasantisation of

Russia's countryside': as sixty years have passed – at least two whole generations – since private agriculture was the rule, the basic skills needed to run a small family farm have been lost, and even the will to resuscitate those skills is absent. There is undoubtedly some truth in this diagnosis. Yet one feels that if the right framework were created, both enterprise and skill could be recovered. This will happen only when villagers are convinced that the party leadership is permanently committed to private farming, and that there will be no more lurches and turn-abouts in policy. Such commitment would require explicitly slimming down collective farms and turning them into co-operatives, while freeing food prices and making cheap credit available to smallholders, as well as investing heavily in rural roads, schools and other services. Only such a demonstrative package of measures would halt the exodus of the best people from the villages and even perhaps promote something of a reverse flow. Gorbachev is still some way short of this kind of commitment. He has shown flexibility and a willingness to learn, but even so, this failing is ominous in a policy area which is crucial if he is to regain the faltering confidence of the public at large, who will assess perestroika not least by what they can buy in their groceries.

The one economic innovation that is producing results is the co-operative sector – essentially the private sector under another name. Dotted around Moscow, and increasingly in other towns as well, are restaurants, hairdressers, fruit and vegetable stalls, shoe repair booths and so on, where the décor is a little more imaginative, the supplies somewhat more reliable, the quality a little higher – and the prices three or four times those prevailing in the state sector. People make use of them, but often they resent them, partly from prejudice, as I have noted above. But they also have some objective reasons for their animosity. As a correspondent recently wrote to *Pravda* from Saratov: 'In the shops everything has vanished, but in the private markets there is more and more. How does it get there? You have to pay 250 to 300 roubles for a pair of women's boots. My daughter needs some, but she earns only 115 roubles a month – where's she supposed to get the money from?'[16]

This is one of those problems which are caused by having to implement the reforms piecemeal and without a secure legal framework. The co-operatives are not yet buttressed by legally protected institutions of private property or by properly worked out commercial and contract law. An alien body in an economy still mainly directed by the state, they inevitably have the air of the parasitical or the criminal, and they charge the high prices necessary to keep an insecure business going. They are able to do this because they have been introduced in conditions of scarcity: they are trading in products whose output has not (or not yet) increased. Many people believe they acquire their wares by entering into agreements with officials in the material-technical supply sector of the planned economy.[17] If that is true, then in effect the co-operatives are aggravating the shortages by sucking goods out of the state sector. In short, the new private economy is conspiring with the old sclerotic public one to profit by the chronic shortages and thus exacerbate them. It is an unhappy result of the first tangible 'success' of the reform. Unfortunately, the state has not been able to respond by stepping up its own output of much-needed consumer goods and services. Instead, in the lingering spirit of perestroika Mark 1, it has merely attempted to restrict by law what co-operatives may do and sell, and the prices they may charge.[18]

The rising prices in the co-operatives fuel people's fears of what may happen if reform bites in the state sector. If the 'dependence economy' is abolished and the huge subsidies for housing, food and transport are withdrawn, then the prices of these basic necessities will rise beyond the reach of the less well paid. They will either become destitute, or their pay will have to be raised proportionately. This would in turn reinforce the inflation which is bound to take hold once restrictions are removed, and the money which people have been saving for lack of anything to spend it on begins to come into circulation in pursuit of perhaps more abundant but still insufficient goods. According to Selyunin, at the beginning of 1988 there were 260 milliard roubles in savings accounts, plus an unknown amount under mattresses: probably in total as much as the annual income of the entire Soviet population.[19]

This kind of inflation is something the authorities dread. The Soviet workers are not quite so docile as is generally assumed in the west. They have occasionally demonstrated and gone on strike, even during the Brezhnev period. The last time they rioted in the streets was, as already mentioned, in 1962, when Khrushchev put up the price of sausage meat by a third without compensating wage rises. The new prices were repealed, and subsidies increased instead – and have been steadily growing to the present day, which suggests that the authorities fear a repetition, a fear doubtless reinforced periodically by events in neighbouring Poland.[20]

So the fate of the Soviet economic reformer is unenviable indeed. He is faced with two alternatives. Either the reforms fail, in which case perestroika as a whole is doomed, and the Soviet Union will probably fall apart and certainly cease to be a great power. Or they will succeed, engendering working-class unrest and ethnic tension to a degree which may well strain the resources of the state. Moreover, the combination of relative political freedom and a high level of information with dis-appointing economic performance (more or less the current juncture in the Soviet Union) has in the past been thought to create a classical revolutionary situation. Even the legendary patience of the Russians may be expected eventually to give way at a time when they are, as we have seen, rediscovering their talent for improvised collective action.

How is one to evaluate perestroika in terms of the Marxist-Leninist ideology Gorbachev professes? At times one is tempted to conclude that he has abandoned ideology altogether. During a visit to Siberia in September 1988, he was confronted by an earnest young man who asked him, 'What stage of socialism have we reached now?' Gorbachev replied disarmingly: 'You've all got used to thinking like this: you're a young fellow, and all you're interested in is stages! [Laughter] I believe we are at the stage of restructuring that which we have so far created. That's the stage we're at.'[21]

This cheerful renunciation of any tangible goal, even of any sense of the forward march of history, must be for old-timers one of the most disconcerting aspects of the world view now being projected in the Soviet media. As Yurii Bondarev (secretary of the RSFSR Writers'

Union) has complained: 'We do not need to destroy our past in order to build our future . . . Could our restructuring be compared to an aircraft which has taken off without knowing whether there is a landing strip at its destination?'[22] It is true that the 'landing strip' has been located in very general terms. The political commentator Fyodor Burlatskii, for example, has suggested that 'socialism has one simple and obvious goal: the welfare and culture of the working man. Everything else – industry and socialisation – is a means to that end.'[23] Nor did Lenin himself ever produce a detailed blueprint of socialist society beyond the vague and non-committal observations contained in *State and Revolution* about a self-administering society in which the exploitation of man by man will have ceased.

So Gorbachev has good authority for the unspecific nature of his vision. One sometimes suspects, indeed, that the invocation of Lenin has become a substitute for clear thinking. The more Gorbachev criticises all the intervening leaders – and with them nine-tenths of Soviet history – the more he needs to cling to the one name which remains inviolate. But his Lenin is selective. The Lenin he quotes is from the period of the transition from War Communism to the New Economic Policy in 1921, when extremes of centralisation and coercion had been shown to lead to social breakdown, when the economy was being freed, culture diversified, and society allowed once more to reveal its tensions and conflicts, simply in order to restore some kind of normality: the first perestroika of Soviet history, in other words. The fact that that same Lenin was simultaneously banning factions and platforms within the party – and thus suppressing serious discussion – is not mentioned.

One notable aspect of Gorbachev's 'socialism' is that it is no longer defined in implacable opposition to 'capitalism'. 'Class struggle' has been sharply downgraded. 'With the emergence of weapons of mass . . . destruction, there appeared an objective limit to class confrontation in the international arena: the threat of universal destruction . . . The backbone of the new way of thinking is the recognition of the priority of human values, or, to be more precise of humankind's survival.'[24]

Of course, the Khrushchev and Brezhnev leaderships had in their own ways also recognised this priority, but they always maintained that the class struggle nevertheless continued. Gorbachev has gone much further than arrangements for mutual survival. He has explicitly declared that in a world of rapid travel and instant mass communications it is hardly possible – or only at ruinous cost – to preserve a closed society. Glaring economic inequality and the threat of a global ecological catastrophe make more concerted international co-operation imperative. [25] As he told a meeting of representatives of culture and the media in January 1989: 'The vital imperative which faces mankind is the priority of all-human values, a world without violence and wars, diversity [*mnogovariantnost'*] of social progress, dialogue and co-operation for the sake of development and the preservation of civilisation, and movement towards a new world order.' [26]

These are not just words: they have led to a palpable reassessment of the Soviet Union's strategic needs, as a result of which it has decided at least to explore the possibility that a less confrontational stance towards the outside world might provide greater security than endless re-arming. Hence the withdrawal from a costly and demoralising war in Afghanistan. Hence also the agreement to scrap intermediate range nuclear missiles, with proper provision of mutual inspection, to reduce strategic arms, and to begin a unilateral reduction in conventional forces both in Europe and on the Chinese frontier. We do not know what the military think of these steps – glasnost does not extend to open debate about them – but they face the west with the embarrassing gratification of seeing many of its own principal demands suddenly conceded by the adversary, a spectacle which promises to bring disarray to the NATO alliance and thus to achieve some of the Soviet Union's more traditional goals as well.

In further pursuit of closer interdependence, the Soviet Union during 1987–8 released most (though not all) of its political prisoners, established its own Human Rights Commission under Fyodor Burlatskii, and took a more open and constructive part in the European Security and Co-operation process, to the extent of offering to host the next major review conference, in 1991. It has simplified travel procedures for its own citizens, so that both personal visits and professional consultations with the outside world have become easier and more frequent. The Soviet Union has in a real sense rejoined the international community.

Both internally and externally, then, 'socialism' has become a much more open and fluid concept. The terms in which it is discussed – decentralisation, pluralism, popular representation, freedom of information and discussion – are more reminiscent of John Stuart Mill than of Karl Marx, and remind one that Marxism is a bastard child of bourgeois liberalism. And indeed a Soviet philosopher has recently argued that when Marxism is expounded rigidly and in rejection of the past, then it naturally engenders Stalinism: it needs to return to its origins. 'We shall create nothing meaningful if we stick to our old conviction that it is only by means of destruction that man will attain happiness. The rule of law is a legacy of bourgeois culture. Freedom of conscience was also born there.'[27]

Vadim Medvedev, head of the Central Committee ideological commission, confirms this openness to the experience of others: 'We cannot indiscriminately brush aside the experience accumulated by capitalism merely on the grounds that it is a different social system . . . This is not just a matter of scientific and technological achievements, but of a whole variety of forms of social organisation, and of solutions to social problems. I believe we shall have to undertake a serious reassessment of the practice of present-day social democracy in defending the social and democratic attainments of working people.'

The heritage of liberalism and social democracy are thus unambiguously on the agenda in developing the new version of socialism. Gorbachev seems, moreover, not averse to observing multi-party variants of it take shape in Hungary and Poland. But he is not disposed to allow this to happen in the Soviet Union itself. In the heartland of socialism there is still a boundary to openness and experiment. At his January 1989 meeting he specifically rejected the idea of a Soviet multi-party system, while Medvedev has asserted that 'socialist pluralism' can be guaranteed with a single party provided that three conditions are present: (i) there exists a multiplicity of organisations and associations to express the full variety of social interests; (ii) the party itself is democratised; and (iii) the rule of law and a high level of culture are firmly entrenched.[28]

So once again we are up against the paradox. Some progress has been made towards all three prerequisites. But they are still very far from being secured. Many social organisations remain unregistered and are sporadically harassed for defending 'social interests'. The undemocratic *nomenklatura* system still dominates appointments, both within the party and to important posts outside it, even though it is to some extent diluted by secret ballots, choice of candidates and limitation of tenure. Most important of all, the rule of law cannot be consolidated while a single party still claims superior wisdom and the right to supervise all social processes. Gorbachev may have recognised the dangers of not having an institutionalised opposition, but all the same, he seems determined to prevent one being established.

So what the Soviet Union has today can at best be described as pluralism under sufferance. Perhaps, however, that is the only way in which pluralism can in practice develop at all inside the Soviet political tradition.

If it is to develop further, then the vital extra ingredient will be the rule of law. This is the cornerstone of the logic of perestroika Mark 2, and also its sharpest break with the past. Traditionally the attitude of the Soviet state towards the law has been ambivalent. On the one hand Marxist theory views the state as the governing committee of the ruling class and law as an instrument by means of which it maintains itself in power; this implies that with the overthrow of all ruling classes and the withering away of the state the law itself is no longer needed. On the other hand, the Soviet state, having conspicuously not withered away under Stalin, has required a normative framework for the regulation of society, and especially to direct the complicated channels of economic planning.

After Stalin's death the law was called in to perform further functions. The party leaders actually had an interest in strengthening legality as a guarantee against the resumption of arbitrary one-man terror, under which all their heads had been at risk. They also regarded law as a means of educating people in their social responsibility and involving them in the process of 'self-administration', which theoretically would eventually become universal and render the state superfluous. At the same time, they did not want to deprive themselves of the judicial weapons on which they were accustomed to rely for the maintenance of their power. So they formalised and propagandised what they called 'socialist legality', while reserving to themselves the right to bend its procedures to their own ends. They made no secret of what they were doing: indeed, in case anyone was in doubt, they specifically rejected the notion of the primacy of the rule of law, and reasserted the party's right to take ultimate decisions. [29]

All the same the concern to preserve juridical decorum created opportunities which, as we have seen, the dissenters used to project their own concept of legality. When the authorities arrested them, they at least had to genuinely try them, however much they distorted court procedures in order to obtain an acceptable verdict. As for the dissenters, their behaviour, in calling on the state to observe its own constitution, meant they had emancipated themselves from the outlook of most Soviet citizens, who helplessly regard law as something to be manipulated by the authorities for their own purposes. They asserted Vladimir Bukovskii's 'small core of freedom in each individual'.

Whether as a result of Soviet legal education, or through western broadcasting of information about the dissenters, I would say that the legal consciousness of many Soviet citizens today – especially educated ones – is higher than we commonly realise, and certainly as high as among my own colleagues in Britain. I find that Soviet friends talking among themselves, even casually, take for granted a knowledge of the constitution, of judicial institutions and of the more frequently applied articles of the Criminal Code. Of course some acquaintance with pass book and residence regulations, or with labour law, is essential just to get by in life, but in my experience nowadays many Soviet citizens are quite searching in their analysis of these enactments: they feel it is worthwhile making a fuss if their rights are infringed, and they know how to go about it. The Soviet people are gradually becoming a nation of barrack-room lawyers, which is a decided advance on their past juridical ignorance and apathy. Indeed, this must be one of the most significant social changes to have taken place in the last generation or so.

Altogether, then, legal awareness is another field in which the political authorities have been lagging behind social consciousness, and have some catching up to do if they are to counteract mounting public cynicism. It is partly a matter of removing vaguely worded laws which can be brought to bear against people inconvenient to local grandees: the parasite law, for instance, which makes it a criminal offence not to be in paid employment, and, like the vagrancy laws of Elizabethan England, can be used to get rid of troublemakers. But partly it is a matter of ensuring that the procuracy and the courts observe their own procedures and are independent of political pressure. Many recent articles by the new breed of Soviet investigative journalist have focused on the phenomenon of 'telephone law', that is, the practice by which party or soviet officials ring up the judge and advise him what the outcome of a particular case should be. Jurists have pondered how judges can be effectively shielded from this kind of pressure, perhaps by lengthening their terms of office, perhaps through having them appointed by superior bodies rather than by the local soviet. Defence counsels have asked for access to their clients at an earlier stage of criminal proceedings, at the beginning of the investigation rather than only at the end of it, to affirm the principle that the accused is presumed innocent until proved guilty and is therefore entitled to competent advice from the outset on how best to present his case.

The 19th Party Conference in July 1988 took up such trivial-looking but actually rather significant minutiae of the legal process and subsumed them under the heading of 'forming the socialist legal state'. 'The law', it declared, 'is paramount in all spheres of society's life.' And the conference resolution added as a gloss: 'It is necessary to give paramount attention to the legal protection of the individual and to consolidate guarantees of the Soviet people's political, economic and social rights and freedoms.'[30]

If those words mean what they say, they are potentially historic. They imply that the ultimate goal of the socialist state is no longer the building of communism, and that the final authority in all questions no longer rests with the party. Furthermore, they state that the individual – and by implication therefore no longer the collective or society as a whole – is the primary focus of the law.

Here the visions of jurists merge with those of writers, scientists, economists, even religious believers, to produce an image of man very different from the 'new Soviet man' projected in the hitherto prevailing ideology. This is where perestroika Mark 2 breaks totally with perestroika Mark 1 – at least if it is followed through to its logical conclusion. In so far as we can define the Communist Party's present vision of socialism, it must be through the laws recently issued and the draft legislation currently being prepared. Under this dispensation the 'new Soviet man Mark 2' will in principle enjoy a whole range of rights and immunities. He will have the right to be a free economic agent within the framework of a family or co-operative business. If he is employed in the state sector, he will be able to elect his superiors and have the right to be consulted about their major decisions. Laws on co-operatives and on the socialist enterprise already extend to him these benefits. He will be able to participate in political life by choosing between different candidates put forward for councils at local, republican and all-Union level; and to exercise this choice responsibly he will have the right to obtain information and openly discuss it with others. The electoral law for the new legislative assemblies already exists, and laws on glasnost and freedom of information are being elaborated. He will be able to join with like-minded fellow citizens in voluntary associations of all kinds, including those designed to agitate for particular political purposes: for this a law on informal associations is pending. He will enjoy freedom of belief and worship, the right to understake charitable activity and perhaps to give religious instruction to his children, depending on the provisions of the law on religious associations currently being drafted. He will be free from arbitrary arrest, his telephone conversations and personal correspondence will be confidential, his home inviolable. As a pledge of this, the Soviet authorities began releasing 'prisoners of conscience' in early 1987; they also announced their intention of bringing legislation into line with international agreements on human rights and of establishing a Human Rights Commission under the authoritative journalist and political scientist Fyodor Burlatskii.

All the same, it would be premature to assume that this vision of the future is assured. None of it is really secure yet. Hanging ominously over all its prospective benefits is the shadow of 'the leading role of the party', which has not only not been renounced, but was explicitly reasserted at the 19th Party Conference. This might not matter so much if the promised 'democratisation' of the party apparatus had taken place, with officials being elected by secret ballot against alternative candidates, and with their terms of office limited to ten years. If carried through, this reform will undermine the *nomenklatura* patronage system and create conditions which will facilitate uninhibited discussion and even the formation of embryonic alternative political groupings within the party. But, by its nature, the reform requires a full decade to implement in full, and the decisive battles for the future of the Soviet Union seem likely to be fought out before then. Khrushchev, who attempted a similar democratisation, was removed long before it could be completed.

Even where it loses in substance, the apparatus likes to record a moral victory. The prisoners released in 1987 were asked to sign statements promising not to 'repeat their offences', and thus implicitly acknowledge that they had been justly sentenced in the first place (some refused to sign, but were released anyway). [31]

Besides, the apparatus still dominates the legislative process. The laws embodying the new civil liberties are being elaborated slowly in the bowels of the bureaucracy, where the domination of the *nomenklatura* is as yet unchallenged. Until the new Supreme Soviet meets, there will be no systematic public discussion of the drafts. Some of the new laws already promulgated have aroused serious public disquiet about how far the authorities intend in practice to observe the promised freedoms. A decree of July 1988 made street demonstrations and public meetings impossible to organise at short notice, and hedged them around with restrictions.[32] (It was under the provisions of this decree that special troops were sent into Tbilisi in April 1989.) No less worrying was an *ukaz* of April 1989 on state crimes: this abolished the old articles 70 and 190 of the Criminal Code, under which human rights activists of the seventies had been sentenced, but still made it a criminal offence to 'call for changes in the political system in a manner contrary to the Constitution' (i.e. by recommending an end to the party's monopoly?), or to 'discredit or insult official institutions' (i.e. by criticising their policies?).[33]

The new political system received its first real trial in the Congress of People's Deputies, which met in May/June 1989. It was constituted in such a way as to ensure the dominance of the apparatus. One-third of the seats were reserved for 'public organisations' – which meant not the informal associations which I have described at length, but rather the established institutions and corporations of Soviet society, such as the Communist Party, the Komsomol, the Council of Soviet Women, and the Council of War and Labour Veterans, all of which are thoroughly penetrated by the *nomenklatura* and its appointees. In many of these institutions, including the Communist Party itself, the election of delegates proceeded in time-honoured fashion through the authoritative nomination of just enough candidates to fill the seats available. Only in a few cases – like, as might be expected, the Academy of Sciences and the creative unions – were there serious and vigorously contested electoral meetings which produced a few oppositional delegates. One of them was Andrei Sakharov, who, however, was finally elected only after a virtual *coup d'état* in the Presidium of the Academy of Sciences.[34]

In the other two-thirds of seats, elected in normal territorial constituencies, electoral commissions could and did arrange procedures in such a way as to discourage unofficial candidates. Denied any access to the curia for 'public organisations', the informal associations had to put forward their candidates for these constituency seats. As we have seen

(Chapter 5), they did remarkably well in a few cases, especially in the Baltic. But overall the domination of the apparatus remained overwhelming: 85 per cent of deputies to the Congress were members of the CPSU – more than was usual in the old unreformed Supreme Soviet. Not that party membership is a fair measure of loyalism, since some elected party members were oppositional in outlook, while some non-party delegates were unswervingly deferential. However one measures it, though, not more than 15 to 20 per cent of deputies could be considered oppositional. [35]

Even this modest admixture made a startling difference from the insipid unanimity of previous Soviet legislative assemblies. As it turned out, the Congress of People's Deputies faithfully reflected the ambiguities of the new political system. Convening without its procedures or even its functions fully worked out, it could be saved from chaos during its first days only by the adroit and authoritarian chairmanship of Gorbachev himself. He handled the procedural wrangles skilfully and forthrightly, intervening in good-humoured manner to put speakers right and even on occasions prompting or correcting the deputy chairmen who stood in for him. More substantial controversies he diverted into 'special commissions' for prolonged examination. It was a virtuoso display of what might be called 'presidential democracy'. In keeping with the new spirit, it did not go unchallenged: several speakers rebuked him for his constant interruptions. [36]

According to the political reform agreed at the 19th Party Conference, the Congress was to meet for only a few days, and its principal duty was to elect the head of state and the 540 delegates to the new-style Supreme Soviet, which was to meet for several months each year and carry out the substantive work of law-making. Even those fundamental parameters were not accepted without question by all deputies. There were a few who felt that, like the Estates General of 1789, the Congress should assume the powers of a sovereign popular assembly. Andrei Sakharov argued at the outset that the Congress should itself take on the supreme law-making function, and not delegate that responsibility to a haphazardly elected one-quarter of its members. [37] He was supported by A. Obolenskii, who proposed that the leading role of the party should be expunged from the constitution, and the slogan 'All power to the Soviets' made into a reality. The Congress should moreover act immediately, he exhorted, for who could be certain that it would not suffer the fate of the Constitutent Assembly in 1918 (which was forcibly dissolved by Lenin before it could hold its second meeting because its elected majority was opposed to Bolshevik rule). [38]

Constitutional controversies of this kind were constantly being inflamed by ethnic tensions. When Gorbachev proposed that a new constitutional control commission should adjudicate on issues of disputed sovereignty between Moscow and the union republics, the Lithuanians walked out in support of their claim that all powers belonged to the republics unless specifically entrusted by agreement to Moscow. To mollify them, a decision had to be delayed, while a special commission was mandated to study the issue, with radical and non-Russian representatives sitting on it. Yet another commission was set up on the insistence of the Balts, to examine the Nazi–Soviet Pact of 1939, and therefore the basis on which rested the Baltic republics' membership of the USSR. [39]

There were sharp disagreements on the crucial matter of the procedure to be adopted in electing the members of the Supreme Soviet. The Lithuanian delegation spoke for many of the non-Russians in urging that those elections should be held in republican and regional caucuses. Otherwise, argued Vitautas Landsbergis, chairman of Sajudis, the Lithuanian delegates would be elected by a vast body of deputies who could not possibly know them individually. 'We are not entitled to vote in the dark,' he proclaimed, and threatened that the Lithuanians would boycott the ballot. This proposal to regionalise the elections was opposed both by the rank-and-file deputies, and by the Russian radicals, who did not want to see the reform drive fragmented and dissipated by ethnic animosities. 'We are not electing the Lithuanian Supreme Soviet, but the USSR Supreme Soviet,' declared the historian Roy Medvedev. [40]

The Moscow radicals were, however, also concerned about the crude majority voting power held by the rump of the deputies, which seemed set to bolster and perpetuate the power of the apparatus under the new system. 'The apparatus has been in power for decades,' stormed economist Gavriil Popov, 'and the leadership has got nowhere as a result of that, except into a blind alley.' He warned that Moscow's scientific and cultural delegates might break away from the rest of the capital city's delegation and vote separately.[41]

The results of the voting were exactly as Popov and his colleagues had feared. The radical Moscow delegates, being conspicuous targets, received a particularly high number of negative votes, and El'tsin failed to be returned. He eventually secured a place in the Supreme Soviet only because another delegate altruistically yielded his seat.[42] The might of the usually silent majority was occasionally made noisily manifest, as when they acclaimed General Rodionov, commander of the troops involved in the Tbilisi massacre, or when they shouted down Sakharov for attacking atrocities committed by the Soviet Army in Afghanistan. In general the apparatus domination of the Supreme Soviet, and therefore of the decisive phase of all Soviet legislation, seems likely to be overwhelming.

All the same, it will not be able to conduct its affairs in the vapid spirit of the past. For if the Congress of People's Deputies carried out its constitutional functions unevenly, it fulfilled its informal ones with sensational success. John Stuart Mill taught that one of the crucial roles of any legislative assembly was to inform the public and stimulate political debate. This the Congress achieved with a vengeance. Operating with greater glasnost than the British House of Commons, it allowed its proceedings to be televised live. From Vil'nyus to Vladivostok, from Arkhangel'sk to Astrakhan', the Soviet peoples were transfixed in front of their television sets, watching the spectacle of their lives, the last and greatest 'return of the repressed'. They saw Egor Ligachev, the party's agricultural chief, ridiculed as a man who had 'failed in ideology' and knew not the first thing about agriculture. They saw the weightlifter Yurii Vlasov denounce the KGB as 'an underground empire stained with blood'. They saw the Minister of the Interior summoned to the rostrum without warning to explain why the police had forcibly broken up a peaceful political meeting in Moscow the previous evening. They saw General Rodionov, commander of the Caucasian Military District, squirming in the face of hostile questions about why his troops had used spades and poison gas to massacre peaceful demonstrators in Tbilisi. And in the evenings Muscovites would leave their televisions and go off to public meetings, at Luzhniki Stadium or elsewhere, to hear their deputies report on the day's speeches and to ask probing questions.[43]

The Supreme Soviet will, in short, not be permitted its traditional comfortable tedium. One of the achievements of the Congress of People's Deputies was to begin the process of crystallising a formal opposition, with its nucleus among the Moscow radicals and the Baltic representatives. They will not be numerous, but they are likely to be vociferous, and they will address the chambers with the confidence that they speak for millions of concerned and politically informed fellow-citizens. As the political scientist L. Batkin has commented, 'A constructive opposition, resting on a mass movement of voters' clubs and people's fronts, is already on the agenda.'[44] When the power of the apparatus is deployed (as it certainly will be) to counteract the rule of law and the exercise of genuine choice, that fact will immediately be registered and made known.

Andrei Sakharov has called Gorbachev's political reform 'a campaign to achieve democratic change by undemocratic means'.[45] That aptly sums up the institutional paradox which was on display at the Congress of People's Deputies, and which is rooted in the Soviet Union's whole past. Leonard Schapiro used to observe, correctly in my view, that the totalitarian state was incompatible with the rule of law and with respect for morality and personal freedom. Yet here we have a General Secretary of the Communist Party who has moved a long way towards the conclusion that, without the rule of law and respect for the individual, his party will be increasingly out of touch with educated people, and the Soviet Union will continue to decline or will even break up. The ultimate implication of what Gorbachev is saying (though he is not yet ready to follow his own logic to the end) is that, to ensure its own power, the party must renounce its political monopoly. No paradox could be more fundamental.

Gorbachev has devised his own solution for bridging the horns of this dilemma. He has upgraded the soviets as a counterweight to the party – and then assumed the leadership of both of them, as President of the Supreme Soviet as well as General Secretary of the Communist Party. Whereas all his predecessors have been chosen by a few colleagues in smoke-filled rooms, he has become under the new electoral system what the Soviet Union has never had before, a popularly elected leader. Armed with a dual mandate, from party and people, he has secured an extra foothold for dealing with those recalcitrant *apparatchiks*.

Here again Gorbachev is advancing towards democracy by undemocratic means. He did not have the grace to wait for the new electoral system before being elevated to the new dual eminence, but had himself made President of the Supreme Soviet under the old discredited system of unanimous show of hands. Also disquieting is the provision that the dual mandate is normally to be held at all levels of the party and the soviets: that is, every district or regional party first secretary will put himself forward for election to the post of chairman of the equivalent soviet. Mind you, after the election campaign of March 1989 one can no longer be certain that they will normally be elected. But, if they are, they will *strengthen* party domination of the soviets, the exact opposite of Gorbachev's declared intentions.

There are, in short, manifest dangers in Gorbachev's new Bonapartism. It will take extraordinary self-restraint on his part not to let his doubly dominant office degenerate into mere despotism – and the means by which he was elected to it were not reassuring. But perhaps all the same for the moment we should give Gorbachev the benefit of the doubt. After all, Napoleon Bonaparte introduced by authoritarian means the first consistent code of laws in France, one which acknowledged individual rights and laid the basis for the gradual evolution of democracy. Besides, authoritarianism which recognises that contradictory and clashing interests exist, and holds them in check, is much preferable to totalitarianism, which tries to pretend they don't exist at all, and smothers them in a blanket of fraudulent propaganda. Preferable, I mean, in the sense that authoritarianism leaves open the possibility of evolution into pluralism, as the recent history of Spain has testified. As for the leading role of the party, probably a good deal of ambiguity, even hypocrisy on that issue can be tolerated for the time being. After all, it took a century or more in Britain for the idea to gain general currency that opposition to His Majesty's Government was not seditious, but an integral part of the working of the constitution. Better that the Communist Party should have ambiguous aims than monolithic ones.

The problem is that Soviet authoritarianism is likely to be unstable. The totalitarian polity does not rest on the long-established institutions and social classes which are likely to have survived in an authoritarian system and which impart a degree of stability to its functioning. The Soviet Union's tenuous traditions of community and participation are of the kind I outlined in Chapter 2. They are not non-existent (as many western observers used to believe), but they do not provide the information, feedback and ongoing support which a flexible and responsive polity requires. Yet the Soviet system boasts the full appurtenances of democracy: a constitution, guarantees of civil rights, legislative assemblies, law courts, the mass media. So far these institutions have been performing a ghostly charade, devoid of real substance. When substance is abruptly restored to them, and the charade all at once becomes genuine politics, then the habits of thought and behaviour are not there to absorb and render tolerable the conflicts which inevitably result. This is most immediately apparent in the ethnic field, and may become so at any time in the economic one.

Theoretically, one might hypothesise a long transitional period during which the 'leading role of the party' afforded a framework for pluralism *de facto* gradually to consolidate itself, rather as it did under the shelter of the monarchy in eighteenth-century Britain. The trouble is, the issues are too urgent, the sources of stability too weak, and the example of existing democracies too conspicuous for such a gentle transition. Whig Britain did not pretend to be a democracy, nor did it have to contend with Radio Free Amsterdam, or have its game laws investigated by human rights commissions from New England. The ethnic and economic problems of the Soviet Union are very pressing and could become interconnected. As I have pointed out, we could well see Russian nationalists mobilising in alliance with conservative *apparatchiks* and perhaps the military or the KGB in order to oppose national breakaway movements and liberal economic reform, and to defend the centrally planned, egalitarian economy and the unitary Soviet empire. Any of the numerous ethnic flashpoints could provide a convenient pretext for a backlash: indeed, it is conceivable that the Tbilisi massacre of April 1989 was a deliberate attempt to provoke a crisis and force Gorbachev to rein back his reform programme.

As if all that were not enough, Eastern Europe is in a precarious and unpredictable condition. On the one hand, developments in Poland and Hungary offer Soviet radicals the possible vision of a multi-party democracy; on the other, both there and in the other countries of the Warsaw Pact there is the risk of political breakdown and popular unrest. Faced with a direct internal threat to the Pact, we cannot yet say whether Gorbachev's 'new thinking' would prevail over old habits, or whether 'fraternal intervention' might not again take place.

Such an eventuality would certainly kill perestroika Mark 2 in the Soviet Union. In those circumstances, Gorbachev (or a possible successor) would probably trim his sails back to perestroika Mark 1. But this could no longer restore quiescence. By now the genie is out of the bottle. Civil society is incomparably more vigorous than it was a mere two short years ago. To hold the multi-national empire together, the authorities would need both to strengthen their coercive apparatus and to institute super-Brezhnevian corruption in a manner which would distract the country from its international priorities and further enfeeble the social fabric. The Soviet Union would return to being a surly and unpredictable power in the international arena, prone to lash out with the armed forces which would be its only glory. Ultimately, too, the problems sidestepped would one day have to be tackled, and the social forces I have described would then reassert themselves, embittered by delay.

On the other hand, there is no doubt that Gorbachev's present policies represent the only hope for the Soviet Union. In a sense, the very depth of the present crisis is a tribute to the extent to which he has already been able to arouse the Soviet peoples from their lethargy, enabling nations and religions to interact with one another, political associations and pressure groups to form. The process is tense and violent because so much has been repressed for so long. Now that such a lot has been achieved, there can be no return to the fraudulent stability of 'stagnation'. Only the rule of law, genuine federalisation and a freer economy can offer a way towards real stability and prosperity.

In the politics of achieving this, I believe it is the Russians themselves who bear the brunt of the responsibility. They must learn greater sensitivity towards the ethnic partners with whom they share their multi-national state. The key figures in the political balance are the Russian nationalists whom I have termed 'revivalists', people like Valentin Rasputin, who care about their culture and environment and worry that they are vulnerable to rock music, pornography, consumerism and all the other western incursions riding on the back of perestroika Mark 2.

Rasputin's speech at the Congress of People's Deputies provided unhappy evidence that he associates these evils, and worse, with the non-Russians of the Soviet Union. Russophobia was stalking the country, he warned, carried by agitators from the Baltic to Georgia, and from there to Armenia and Azerbaijan. 'Anti-Soviet slogans join with anti-Russian ones,' he challenged them, accusing the Balts of preparing to secede from the Soviet Union. 'You want great upheavals, but we want a great country!' His words were those of Stolypin, Russia's Prime Minister, challenging the revolutionaries in the Second Duma of 1907.[46]

Not that Rasputin is in any normal sense a spokesman for the apparatus. In the same speech he condemned the war in Afghanistan and reviled the 'oppression of the administrative-industrial machine, which has proved to be more terrible than the Mongol yoke and has humiliated and plundered Russia as much as anywhere else'. Yet if Rasputin is to follow the logic of his own warnings, then he will find himself allied with the *apparatchiks* and Disgusted Sverdlovsk, defending the integrity of the empire. He will be delivering himself up to Minvodkhoz and the military-industrial complex which he execrates.

In a sense, the fault line in Soviet politics passes right through Rasputin. Perhaps this division reflects the duality of the peasant community which is his ideal, and which, as we have seen, on the one hand exemplified sturdy self-reliance and democratic decision-making, on the other let itself be used as an instrument of patriarchal and arbitrary rule. Both tendencies are present in Russian political culture, but it is crucial today that the former should triumph over the latter. As long as Russians allow themselves to be the bearers of oppressive centralised rule over the other nations of the Soviet Union, then they too will be oppressed, and will not enjoy genuine civil liberty or even the unimpaired expression of their own national aspirations. Whether or not they recognise it, the interests of Russian patriots lie not in alliance with the party-state apparatus, but with Sajudis and the Ukrainian Culturological Club.

But, as the examples of Sergei Zalygin or Academician Dmitrii Likhachev show, there is no ineluctable force binding Russian patriots with the neo-Stalinists. Russians too carry the germ of freedom in their heritage. Admittedly it has at times been deeply buried, in the ambiguous traditions of the peasant community and the intellectuals' *kruzhok*. But the last couple of years have shown beyond doubt not only that it can be revived, but that it can become a real factor in the political life of the country. The prospects for developing it further and building a genuine civil society have, despite all the difficulties, never been more favourable than at the present. If the Russians can play their part in creating that society, then the Soviet Union has both abundant natural resources and a highly trained and educated population: it could, just *could*, become the economic miracle of the twenty-first century. In a country which already has a humane and sophisticated culture, that is certainly a prospect worth working for.

Postscript

The penalty and excitement of writing a work of contemporary history is that one's subject matter changes as one writes. Even as this book has been in press, for example, glasnost has taken a major new step forward with the publication of a novel by Vasilii Grossman which directly accuses Lenin of having created the essentials of the system Stalin later employed for mass murder. The announcement that Solzhenitsyn's works are to be published, including *The Gulag Archipelago*, seals this radicalisation of historical controversy. Solzhenitsyn's view is the same as Grossman's, and it is expressed more vehemently and at greater length. The re-examination of the Soviet past is reaching the point at which glasnost becomes freedom of speech. The polemics thus stirred up are likely to prove lively. Already Russian nationalists (again in tacit solidarity with the conservative sectors of the apparatus) have bitterly attacked Grossman for his assertion that the characteristic features of Russian society are domination and slavery, and that these fatally adulterated Lenin's idealism with murderous fanaticism.

Such unrestrained debate on the fundamentals of the Soviet system is only one indication that I observed during a visit to Moscow and Riga in September 1989 of a qualitatively new stage being reached in the painful and conflict-ridden development of a civil society in the Soviet Union. Indeed, it would not be too much to say that the changes in the political system over the previous six months have been more far-reaching than any since the death of Stalin.

One of the clearest signs of this turbulent self-emancipation is the formation in the Congress of People's Deputies of a coherent opposition group led by Boris El'tsin. Its name, the Inter-Regional Group of Deputies, is not as insipid as it sounds: it indicates that, despite the difficulties I referred to earlier, radical deputies from Moscow have been able to find common ground with their colleagues from the Russian provinces and from some of the non-Russian republics – notably the Baltic – on the need for faster progress towards a pluralist political system, guarantees of human rights, a substantial private sector in the economy, and a federation based on a new treaty between the Union republics. How coherent the Inter-Regional Group will prove in practice remains to be seen, but it aims to publish a regular broadsheet and to establish a political fund for the collection and storing of socio-political information and the drafting of alternative versions of law.

Even if it works as planned, this group is far from being an opposition party in the western sense. It aims to monitor and to put pressure on the existing government, not to form an alternative one. It is a purely parliamentary caucus, without any branches in the country at large. But this 'defect' is in effect being remedied by the formation of supporters' clubs and electoral blocs in the localities, based on the Popular Fronts. By a sort of osmosis, in fact, the informal associations are gradually being drawn into pacts and federations which feed directly into the central political system. They are preparing to maintain and extend the tangible success they achieved in the March 1989 elections. In September 1989 I witnessed a large meeting at Moscow University in which representatives of numerous associations met with deputies from local soviets and with members of the Inter-Regional Group to form an electoral bloc. They discussed heatedly the problems of co-ordinating preparations for the forthcoming local elections, and of putting forward proposals for amendments to an electoral law which is still designed to ensure apparatus domination of the legislature.

It is not certain at the moment how far this process of political alliance formation can go. Once they start to adopt full scale programmes for legislative action, it will become clear that there are serious divergences of outlook among the political activists drawn into the magnetic field of the Inter-Regional Group. At least three tendencies are already evident, at least in Moscow: the anarchists, who believe in a decentralised form of government based on the local soviets, and an economy resting on co-operative property; the social democrats, whose model is a Scandinavian-style political system, with a mixed economy and an extensive state welfare system; and the liberals, who wish to see private property and minimal state interference as the foundation of the economy, combined with an emphasis on human rights and political pluralism.

There are differences not only on the ideal future, but also on the path which might lead to it. As it happens, the crystallisation of opposition forces in the Soviet Union has coincided with profoundly significant developments in the state socialist societies of Eastern Europe, which offer two divergent models of how to proceed. In what might be called the 'Polish variant', the party apparatus is seen as a monolithic entity, hostile to reform, so that decisive change can only be brought about by organising the working people in massive strikes and demonstrations. In the 'Hungarian variant', the apparatus is seen as split, and the emerging opposition aims to ally itself with its reformist wing in order to effect peaceful reform by legislative means. If both models fail, then pessimists discern a third variant, the 'Chinese' one, after the June massacre in Tienanmen Square.

The summer of 1989 saw a whole new social class take a first step towards civil society – in one sense the most significant and certainly the most numerous of all the classes of Soviet society, namely the industrial workers. The continuities of Russian history were abundantly in evidence when the coalminers of Siberia and the Donbass went on strike. Like the soviets of 1905, the strike committees of 1989 were elected by the workers at their workplace in defiance of official institutions, put forward their demands, negotiated with the employers and the authorities, and helped to keep order in their towns during the strike. They even enforced a rigid ban on alcohol, to minimise the chance of fortuitous ugly confrontations. As well as calling for better working conditions, housing, food supplies and medical care (all matters that arouse deep resentment among workers who feel that the apparatus has cheated them of their heritage), they also made political demands: for the removal of particularly objectionable officials, for a say in the running of their own pits and for the right to their own trade unions independent of the official ones. The strike committees formed regional federations to strengthen their hand, called on the Supreme Soviet for help (a reflection of the prestige the new legislature already enjoys) and remained in being after the return to work, to monitor the implementation of the settlements, and to continue to represent the workers. Strike committees even appeared in factories and regions where there were no strikes! There could be no more telling indication of the workers' long pent-up need to feel themselves able to take action on their own behalf, and of their ability to do so.

The various nations of the Soviet Union continue, in different ways, to flex their muscles and assert their right to their own kind of politics. Sporadic fighting has been going on between the Abkhazians and Georgians, and also between the Armenians and Azerbaijanis. In the latter case, indeed, the Azerbaijanis imposed a blockade on the Armenian Republic in pursuit of their claim to have the special status of Nagornyi Karabakh lifted and the region returned to them. Arkadii Volskii, head of the special administration in Karabakh, spoke openly of the danger of a civil war between the two nations.

The Moldavians, hitherto fairly docile, have created a mass movement which has successfully demanded the abandonment of the Cyrillic alphabet that used to symbolise their language's separation from Romanian. The Baltic Popular Fronts, stimulated by the move towards economic self-regulation and by official revelations about the secret protocols of the Nazi–Soviet Pact, have been tempted to espouse the slogans of their more radical fringes and to try for complete independence from the Soviet Union. At the time of writing, the Latvian Popular Front has written secession into its draft programme, which is due to be debated at a congress. In reaction, both in Moldavia and in the Baltic, Russians have been organising strikes to protest against what they see as the increasing discrimination against them by locals. For its part, the CPSU Central Committee has issued a sharp warning against 'extremism' and 'separatism', which it denounces as 'anti-socialist' and 'anti-Soviet': this regression to the abusive and peremptory style of an earlier era is a reminder that the CPSU has not renounced its responsibility for upholding the integrity of the Soviet Union.

In the teeth of resistance from their local party apparatchiks, both the Belorussians and the Ukrainians have at last succeeded in creating their own Popular Fronts, though the Belorussians were only able to do so by taking refuge in premises offered to them by their neighbours in Lithuania. The Ukrainian Front, known as Rukh, is a particularly significant development, because of the size and key position of Ukraine. Its creation was a personal triumph over Shcherbitskii, who soon resigned as first secretary of the Ukrainian Communist Party and forfeited his position as the last Brezhnevite survivor in the Politburo.

These developments are all increasing society's independence from the overbearing political monopoly which has hitherto dominated it. But they are doing so in ways which intensify conflict, or at least make it manifest where it had been latent. A society which has been so sick for so long cannot recover its health without going through very serious crises. A sense of foreboding and unease is widespread today, caused by economic dislocation, and the growth of crime and ethnic conflict on a scale not seen in most people's lifetimes. Even those who approve of what Gorbachev is doing tend to see him as a man who has undertaken a superhuman task and is being overwhelmed by it. To many, especially among the working class, he is yet another leader who makes fine promises and then fails to live up to them. The greater the discrepancy between words and deeds, the greater the embitterment.

The Soviet Union is today in a critical situation. The rule of the party-state apparatus is breaking down, but as yet nothing has replaced it, even though, as we have seen, the elements of a pluralist political system are taking shape. Gorbachev's reform programme remains plagued by the contradictions inherent in a totalitarian party's attempt to transform itself into something else, as yet unspecified. The economy remains in a limbo between Gosplan and the free market, because the party lacks the conviction to introduce the unambiguous concept of private property. Enterprise law, land law, co-operative law are all weakened by the uncertainties and inconsistencies which result, while corruption and crime flourish on them.

The Union's nations are restless, torn between infinite aspiration and the constraints of reality in a one-party state. A new federal framework for them has been promised but not defined, and the long-awaited Central Committee plenum of September 1989 was a disappointment to them, since it envisaged a federation whose features are laid down by Moscow, not by treaty between nominally sovereign republics. The plenum insisted, moreover, that the Communist Party should remain centralised, not break up into self-governing units at the republican level, as the Lithuanians demanded.

Gorbachev's policies, then, continue to be obstructed not only by objective difficulties, but also by the legacy of the totalitarian past. For the first time in Soviet history, however, there are real political forces in play, both at the centre and in the republics, ready and able to challenge the party's lingering monopoly. One regards the future with both hope and foreboding.

Notes

NB *RL* = Radio Liberty Research Report
    SWB = Summary of World Broadcasts (BBC monitoring service)

1 A great power in crisis

1 *Pravda*, 26 August 1988, p. 1
2 L. Karpinskii, 'Pochemu stalinizm ne skhodit so stseny?' in Yu. N.
  Afanas'ev (ed.), *Inogo de dano* (Moscow, Progress, 1988), p. 655
3 Paul Kennedy, *The Rise and Fall of the Great Powers* (London, Unwin
  Hyman, 1988), p. 515
4 'Appeal of Soviet scientists to the party-government leaders of the USSR',
  Survey, 70 (1970), pp. 160–70
5 Figures extrapolated from: B. Kerblay, *Modern Soviet Society* (London,
  Methuen, 1983), p. 55; F. Starr, 'The Soviet Union: a civil society' in
  Foreign Policy, 70 (spring 1988), p. 27
6 L. A. Anokhina & M. N. Shmelyova, *Byt gorodskogo naseleniya srednei
  polosy RSFSR v proshlom i nastoyashchem* (Moscow, Nauka, 1977), pp.
  58–9
7 *Narodnoe khozyaistvo SSSR v 1985g: statisticheskii ezhegodnik* (Moscow,
  Finansy i Statistika, 1986), pp. 27–30
8 Kerblay, p. 213
9 Starr, p. 30
10 *Ibid.*, p. 27
11 For the theory of totalitarianism, see especially: Carl Friedrich &
  Zbigniew Brzezinski, *Totalitarian Dictatorship and Autocracy*
  (Cambridge, Massachusetts, Harvard University Press, 1956); and
  Leonard Schapiro, *Totalitarianism* (London, Pall Mall, 1972)

12 See the discussion in Susan Solomon (ed.), *Pluralism in the Soviet Union: essays in honour of Gordon Skilling* (London, Macmillan, 1983)

13 See the excellent analysis by Albert Gleeson, '"Totalitarianism" in 1984', *Russian Review*, 43 (1984), pp. 145–59

14 Richard Pipes, 'Can the Soviet Union reform?' in *Foreign Affairs*, 63:1 (fall 1984), p. 49

15 Julia Wishnevsky, 'Soviet television discusses Stalin's legacy', *RL*, 205:88, 17 May 1988

16 Robert Conquest, *The Great Terror* (London, Macmillan, 1968), p. 533. Roy Medvedev, who has spent much of his life gathering material about Stalin (though he was not till recently permitted to publish any of it in the Soviet Union), estimates the number of those 'illegally repressed' throughout his leadership at 40 million. It is clear that a very substantial proportion of those died. *Argumenty i fakty*, 4 February 1989

17 Boris Pasternak, *An Essay in Autobiography* (London, Collins Harvill, 1959), pp. 119–20

18 Varlam Shalamov, *Kolymskie rasskasy* (London, Overseas Publications Interchange, 1978), p. 220

19 Some of them have been published in English in two selections: *Kolyma Tales*, 1980; and *Graphite*, 1981, both published by W. W. Norton of New York

20 A. Zinoviev, *Zheltyi dom* (Lausanne, L'Age d'Homme, 1980), 1, p. 48

21 Vladimir Voinovich, *The Life and Extraordinary Adventures of Private Ivan Chonkin* (London, Jonathan Cape, 1977), p. 145

22 R. H. McNeal (ed.), *Resolutions and Decisions of the Communist Party of the Soviet Union 1898–1964* (Toronto University Press, 1974), 2, pp. 97–8

23 M. Voslensky, *Nomenklatura: anatomy of the Soviet ruling class* (London, Bodley Head, 1984)

24 Marshall I. Goldman, *USSR in Crisis: the failure of an economic system* (New York, W. W. Norton, 1983), p. 86

2 Communities and ideals in Russian society

1 For a view of the origins of this spirit in Muscovy, see Edward Kennan, 'Muscovite political folkways', *Russian Review*, 45:2 (April 1986), pp. 115–82

2 S. G. Pushkarev, *Krest'yanskaya pozemel'no-peredel'naya obshchina v Rossii* (Newtonville, Massachusetts, Oriental Research Partners, 1976);

B. Mironov, 'The Russian peasant commune after the reforms of the 1860s', *Slavic Review*, 44 (1985), pp. 438–67

3 M. M. Gromyko, *Traditsionnye normy povedeniya i formy obshcheniya russkikh krest'yan XIX veka* (Moscow, Nauka, 1986)

4 Stepniak, *The Russian Peasantry*, 2nd edn (London, 1905), p. 636

5 R. E. Zelnik (ed.), *A Radical Worker in Tsarist Russia: the autobiography of Semyon Ivanovich Kanatchikov* (Stanford University Press, 1986), p. 9

6 Solomon Schwarz, *The Russian Revolution of 1905: the workers' movement and the formation of Bolshevism and Menshevism* (University of Chicago Press, 1967), pp. 135–8, 335–8; Abraham Ascher, *The Revolution of 1905: Russia in disarray* (Stanford University Press, 1988), pp. 145–50

7 Teodor Shanin, *Russia 1905–7: revolution as a moment of truth* (London, Macmillan, 1986), ch. 3, especially pp. 89–90; Graeme Gill, *Peasants and Government in the Russian Revolution* (London, Macmillan, 1979), pp. 154–7

8 Alexander Rabinowitch, *The Bolsheviks Come to Power* (London, New Left Books, 1979)

9 Sheila Fitzpatrick, *The Russian Revolution* (London, Oxford University Press, 1982); Robert Service, *The Bolshevik Party in Revolution: a study in organisational change, 1917–23* (London, Macmillan Press, 1979)

10 For a statistical analysis of the urbanisation process and its effects on mentality, see Part One of Moshe Lewin, *The Gorbachev Phenomenon: a historical interpretation* (London, Radius, 1988)

11 Merle Fainsod, *How Russia is Ruled*, revised edn (Cambridge, Massachusetts, Harvard University Press, 1965), pp. 236–7

12 J. S. Berliner, *Factory and Manager in the USSR* (Cambridge, Massachusetts, Harvard University Press, 1957), pp. 243–7, 259–63

13 Alexander Zinoviev, *The Reality of Communism* (London, Victor Gollancz, 1984), p. 72

14 *Ibid.*, p. 92

15 *Ibid.*, p. 114

16 See his article of that title in *Survey*, 26:1 (spring 1982), pp. 28–48

17 Gregory Freeze, *The Russian Levites: parish clergy in the eighteenth century* (Cambridge, Massachusetts, Harvard University Press, 1977); and *The Parish Clergy in Nineteenth Century Russia: crisis, reform and counter-reform* (Princeton University Press, 1983)

18 Daniel Brower, *Training the Nihilists: education and radicalism in Tsarist Russia* (Ithaca, NY, Cornell University Press, 1975)

19 Richard F. Gustafson, *Leo Tolstoy – Resident and Stranger: a study in fiction and theology* (Princeton University Press, 1986), p.xii

20 V. G. Belinsky, 'Thoughts and notes on Russian literature', in his *Selected Philosophical Works* (Moscow, Foreign Languages Publishing House, 1948), p.339

21 From 'Byloe i dumy', *Polnoe sobranie sochinenii* (Moscow, 1919), 12, p.106

22 N. Valentinov, *Encounters with Lenin* (London, Oxford University Press, 1968), p.64

23 N. Bukharin & E. Preobrazhensky, *ABC of Communism* (Harmondsworth, Pelican Books, 1969), p.300

24 Naum Jasny, *Soviet Industrialization, 1928–52* (Chicago University Press, 1961), p.73

25 David Joravsky, *The Lysenko Affair* (Cambridge, Massachusetts, Harvard University Press, 1970); for the situation of the intelligentsia under Stalin, see Boris Kagarlitsky, *The Thinking Reed: intellectuals and the Soviet state, 1917 to the present* (London, Verso, 1988), Ch.3

26 Geoffrey Hosking, 'The institutionalisation of Soviet literature', in G. A. Hosking & G. F. Cushing (eds), *Perspectives on Literature and Society in Eastern and Western Europe* (London, Macmillan, 1989), pp.55–75

27 Hans Günther, *Die Verstaatlichung der Literatur* (Stuttgart, J. B. Metzler Verlag, 1984)

3 The return of the repressed

1 Raisa Orlowa & Lew Kopelew, *Wir lebten in Moskau* (Munich, Albrecht Knaus Verlag, 1987), p.28

2 Gerald Stanton Smith, *Songs to Seven Strings: Russian guitar poetry and Soviet 'mass song'* (Bloomington, Indiana University Press, 1984)

3 Lyudmila Alekseeva, *Istoriya inakomysliya v SSSR: noveishii period* (Benson, Vermont, Khronika Press, 1984), p.247

4 Vladimir Bukovskii, *To Build a Castle: my life as a dissenter* (London, Andre Deutsch, 1978), pp.191–2

5 Alekseeva, p.251

6 Mark Hopkins, *Russia's Underground Press: the Chronicle of Current Events* (New York, Praeger, 1983), p.6

7 *Ibid.*, p.148

8 *Ibid.*, pp.xix–xx

9 V. Haynes & O. Semyonova, *Workers Against the Gulag* (London, Pluto Press, 1979)

10 Alekseeva, pp. 386–8
11 Peter Reddaway (ed.), *Uncensored Russia* (London, Jonathan Cape, 1972), p. 23
12 B. Shragin, 'Oppozitsionnye nastroeniya v nauchnykh gorodkakh', *SSSR: vnutrennie protivorechiya*, 1 (1981), pp. 100–19
13 Ann Shukman, *Literature and Semiotics: a study of the writings of Yu. M. Lotman* (Amsterdam, North Holland Publishing Company, 1977), Ch. 1
14 See Alec Nove's introduction to A. Aganbegyan, *The Challenge: economics of perestroika* (London, Hutchinson, 1988); for further discussion of such 'intra-structural dissent' see Alexander Shtromas, 'Dissent and political change in the USSR', Erik P. Hoffmann and Robbin F. Laird (eds), *The Soviet Polity in the Modern Era* (New York, Aldine Publishing Co., 1984), pp. 727–33
15 V. Lakshin, *Solzhenitsyn, Tvardovsky and Novy Mir* (Cambridge, Massachusetts, MIT Press, 1980), pp. 80–1
16 L. Labedz (ed.), *Solzhenitsyn: a documentary record* (London, Allen Lane, 1970), pp. 15–16; on the applicability of Freudian theory to the Soviet literary situation, see Sidney Monas, 'Censorship as a way of life', in G. A. Hosking & G. F. Cushing (eds), *Perspectives on Literature and Society in Eastern and Western Europe* (London, Macmillan, 1989), pp. 7–22

4 A civil society in embryo

1 *Pravda*, 10 May 1987, p. 3
2 Boris Komarov, *Unichtozhenie prirody* (Frankfurt am Main, Posev, 1978), p. 73
3 V. Chivilikhin, 'Svetloe oko Sibiri', *Oktyabr'*, 4/63, pp. 151–72
4 *Komsomol'skaya pravda*, 11 May 1966; A. Babyonyshev (ed.), *On Sakharov* (New York, Vintage Books, 1982), p. xxi
5 Conversation with V. Rasputin, 31 May 1988; Charles E. Ziegler, *Environmental Policy in the USSR* (London, Frances Pinter, 1987), pp. 53–7
6 V. Rasputin, 'Kak tam, na slavnom more?' *Literaturnaya gazeta*, 24 August 1988, pp. 1–2
7 Thane Gustafson, *Reform in Soviet Politics* (Cambridge University Press, 1981), p. 61
8 Komarov, Ch. 4
9 Gustafson, p. 46

10 Violet Connolly, 'Turning the rivers of Siberia in their courses', *RL* 189/78, 29 August 1978

11 *Russkaya mysl'*, 15 July 1982, pp. 10–11

12 *Literaturnaya gazeta*, 2 July 1986

13 Interview with Professor O. Kolbasov, expert on environmental law at the Institute of State and Law, 15 April 1988

14 Sergei Zalygin, 'Povorot: uroki odnoi diskussii', *Novyi Mir*, 1/87, pp. 3–18; Nicolai N. Petro, 'The project of the century', *Studies in Comparative Communism*, 20:3–4 (autumn/winter 1987), pp. 235–52

15 *Pravda*, 20 May 1988

16 Victor G. Snell, 'The cause of the Chernobyl accident', in David Marples, *The Social Impact of the Chernobyl Disaster* (London, Macmillan, 1988)

17 Victor Haynes & Marko Bojcun, *The Chernobyl Disaster* (London, Hogarth Press, 1988) Ch. 6

18 Marples, pp. 114–15; Haynes & Bojcun, Ch. 5

19 *Moscow News*, 7, 14 February 1988, p. 10

20 Ales' Adamovich, '"Chestnoe slovo, ne vzorvyotsya", ili mnenie nespetsialista', *Novyi Mir*, 9/88, p. 169

21 *Ibid.*, p. 164

22 Bohdan Nahaylo, 'Non-Russian national democratic movements hold another meeting', *RL* 465/88, 10 October, 1988; David Marples, 'New protests against Soviet nuclear energy programme', *RL* 448/88, 28 September 1988

23 Marples, 'New Protests . . .', *RL*, 448/88, p. 4

24 Material on the Trust Group is drawn from Olga Medvedkov, 'The Moscow Trust Group: an uncontrolled grassroots movement in the Soviet Union', *Mershon Centre Quarterly Report* (Ohio State University), 12:4 (spring 1988)

25 *Izvestiya*, 20 May 1988, p. 3

26 *Literaturnaya gazeta*, 25 June 1986, p. 6

27 Bill Keller, *International Herald Tribune*, 8 February 1988, p. 2

28 According to an opinion poll conducted by its own research institute: '"Neformaly" – synov'ya ili pasynki?', *Politicheskoe obrazovanie*, 7/88, p. 83

29 I. Yu. Sundiev, 'Neformal'nye molodyozhnye ob"edineniya: opyt ekspozitsii', *Sotsiologicheskie issledovaniya*, 5/87, pp. 56–62; M. Malyutin, 'Neformaly v perestroike: opyt i perspektivy', in Yu. Afanas'ev (ed.), *Inogo ne dano* (Moscow, Progress, 1988), pp. 216–17

30 *Pravda*, 1 February 1988, p.4; 10 February 1989, p.1; A. Maisenya, 'Kto oni, "neformaly"?', *Sovetskaya Belorussiya*, 1 October 1987, p.4; *Argumenty i fakty*, 31/88, 30 July 1988, pp.6–7

31 *Politicheskoe samoobrazovanie*, 7/88, p.85

32 *Russkaya mysl'*, 18 September 1987, p.5; Alan Bookbinder *et al.*, *Comrades* (London, BBC Publications, 1985), pp.159–60

33 Vera Tolz, 'Informal groups in the USSR', *RL* 220/87, 11 June 1987; K. Sochnev, 'Nevostrebovannye lyudi', *Sel'skaya molodyozh'*, 6/88, pp.8–10

34 Malyutin, p.218

35 Interviews with Grigorii Pel'man, 18 April and 5 May 1988; Nick Lampert, 'Russia's new democrats: the club movement and perestroika', *Detente*, 9–10 (1987), p.10

36 Interview with Grigorii Pel'man, 5 May 1988; Lampert, pp.10–11

37 *The Friend*, 13 May 1988, p.595; 'Informatsionnyi byulleten'' SMOT', no.7, June 1988, *Materialy samizdata*, AS 6300, p.41

38 *Russkaya mysl'*, 19 February 1988; *Materialy samizdata*, AS 6015, pp.39–45; interview with Vyacheslav Igrunov of Perestroika-88, 22 April 1988

39 Interview with Aleksandr Podrabinek, 18 April 1988

40 *Glasnost'*, 2–4, p.2, published as an appendix to *Russkaya mysl'*, 24 July 1987

41 *Zhurnal zhurnalov*, 1, in *Materialy samizdata* AS 6132

42 Boris Kagarlitskii, *The Thinking Reed: intellectuals and the Soviet state, 1917 to the present* (London, Verso Books, 1988); Vera Tolz, 'Informal groups hold first officially sanctioned conference', *RL* 380/87, 23 September 1987; L. Alekseeva, 'Obshchestvennye ob"edineniya v SSSR', *SSSR: vnutrennie protivorechiya*, 21 (1988), pp.90–4

43 Conversation with Boris Kagarlitskii, 15 April 1988; *Komsomol'skaya pravda*, 31 January 1988

44 Vera Tolz, 'Informal groups in the USSR in 1988', *RL* 487/88, 30 October 1988, pp.6–7; B. Kurashvili, *Bor'ba s byurokratizmom* (Moscow, Znanie, 1988), pp.55–6

45 *Ogonyok*, 34/88, 20 August 1988, pp.25–7

46 *Moskovskie novosti*, 23, 5 June 1988, p.15; SWB SU/0172, 8 June 1988, p.i

47 *Posev*, 3/88, pp.4–7

48 *Independent*, 31 March 1989, p.10; *Russkaya mysl'*, 7 April 1989, p.1

49 *Independent*, 29 March 1989, p.12

50 M. Malyutin, 'Nechto o vyborakh ili tret'ya volna', *Otkrytaya zona*, 9 (April 1989), pp.147–50

51 N. Andreeva, 'Ne mogu postupat'sya printsipami', *Sovetskaya Rossiya*, 13 March 1988
52 *SWB* SU/0191, 30 June 1988, C/25
53 *Guardian*, 9 May 1988; *Le Monde*, 11 May 1988
54 Jonathan Aves, 'The Democratic Union – Soviet opposition party?' in *Slovo*, 1:2 (November 1988), p.94
55 Aves, *loc. cit.*; Nicolai Petro, 'Perestroika from below: voluntary socio-political associations in the USSR' (University of Pennsylvania: Foreign Policy Research Institute Paper, March 1989), pp.20–24

5 The flawed melting pot

1 Gail Lapidus, 'Ethnonationalism and stability: the Soviet case', *World Politics*, 36 (1983–4), pp.555–80; Mary McAuley, 'Nationalism and the Soviet multi-ethnic state', in Neil Harding (ed.), *The State in Socialist Society* (London, Macmillan, 1984), pp. 179–210; Roman Karklins, *Ethnic Relations in the USSR* (Boston, Massachusetts, Allen & Unwin, 1986); Alexander J. Motyl, *Will the non-Russians rebel? State, ethnicity and stability in the USSR* (Ithaca, NY, Cornell University Press, 1987)
2 Ernest Gellner, *Nations and Nationalism* (Oxford, Basil Blackwell, 1983), pp.43–50
3 V. I. Kozlov, *Natsional'nosti SSSR: etnodemografischeskii obzor*, (Moscow, Finansy i statistika, 1982), pp.240–1
4 From the protest document of autumn 1987, quoted in *Radio Free Europe Research*, RAD Background Report, 39, 11 March 1988, p.1
5 Tamara Dragadze, 'The Armenian-Azerbaijani conflict: structure and sentiment', *Third World Quarterly*, 11:1 (January 1989), pp.63–5
6 Dragadze, p.62; Lyudmila Alekseeva, *Istoriya inakomysliya v SSSR: noveishii period* (Benson, Vermont, Khronika Press, 1984), pp.83–95
7 *Soviet Analyst*, vol. 17, no. 3, 10 February 1988, pp.1–2
8 *Posev*, 4/88, p.10; *Sunday Times*, 28 February 1988, pp.1, 13.
9 *SWB* SU/0210, 22 July 1988, B/16–17
10 Dragadze, pp.67–9; S. Enders Wimbush, 'Divided Azerbaijan: nation-building, assimilation and mobilisation between three states', in W. O. McCagg, Jr & Brian D. Silver (eds), *Soviet Asian Ethnic Frontiers* (New York, Pergamon Press, 1979), pp.61–82
11 Ronald Grigor Suny, *The Making of the Georgian Nation* (London, Tauris, 1989), Chs.1–3
12 Robert Parsons, 'Informal organisations in Georgia', paper presented to

the Georgian Study Group at the School of Oriental & African Studies, University of London, 5 May 1989

13 Elizabeth Fuller, 'Independent political groupings in Georgia', *RL* 527/88, 25 November 1988

14 *The Times*, 10 April 1989, p. 1; *Sunday Times*, 16 April 1989, p. B1

15 *SWB*, SU/0436, 17 April 1989, B/3

16 Alexander Shtromas, 'The Baltic States', in R. Conquest (ed.), *The Last Empire: nationality and the Soviet future* (Stanford, California, Hoover Institution Press, 1986), pp. 183–217

17 N. R. Miuzneks, 'The Daugavpils hydro-station and glasnost in Latvia', *Journal of Baltic Studies*, 18:1 (spring 1987), pp. 63–70

18 *Radio Free Europe Research*, 13:26, 3 June 1988, pp. 3, 13–14

19 *RFER*, Baltic Area Situation Report 7, 15 July 1988, pp. 15–19

20 *RFER*, Baltic Area Situation Report 5, 20 May 1988, pp. 7–10; *SWB* SU/0251, 8 September 1988, B/3; *SWB* SU/0305, 10 November 1988, B/1–8

21 *Narodnyi Front Latvii: programma, ustav* (Riga, Arots, 1988)

22 *SWB* SU/0205, 16 July 1988, B/3–5

23 Alexander Rahr, 'Lithuanian party leadership demands more autonomy', *RL* 499/88, 8 November 1988

24 Rupert Cornwell, *Independent*, 24 October 1988, p. 1

25 Interview with Anatolii Belaichuk of the Latvian International Front, Novosti Press Agency report of 28 April 1989

26 Associated Press, 14 March 1989

27 *SWB* SU/0393, 24 February 1989, B/4–5

28 Roman Szporluk, 'The Ukraine and Russia', in R. Conquest (ed.), *The Last Empire*; Bohdan Krawchenko, *Social Change and National Consciousness in Twentieth-Century Ukraine* (London, Macmillan, 1985)

29 Roman Solchanyk, 'Statistical *glasnost*': data on language and education in Ukraine', *RL* 152/87, 15 April 1987, p. 2

30 Roman Solchanyk, 'Catastrophic language situation in major Ukrainian cities', *RL* 286/87, 15 July 1987

31 Bohdan Nahaylo, 'Mounting opposition in the Ukraine to nuclear energy programme', *Radio Liberty Supplement* 1/88, 16 February 1988

32 Bohdan Nahaylo, 'Informal Ukrainian Culturological Club helps to break new ground for *glasnost*'', *RL* 57/88, 8 February 1988; interview with Vyacheslav Chornovil and Oles' Shevchenko, 25 April 1988

33 *Russkaya mysl*', 29 July 1988, p. 2

34 Ukrainian Press Agency: Press Release no. 180, 19 November 1988;
no. 183, 8 December 1988; David Marples, 'Mass demonstration in Kiev
focuses on ecological issues and political situation in the Ukraine', *RL*
525/88, 5 December 1988

35 *Literaturna Ukraina*, 16 February 1989, quoted in *SWB* SU/0403,
8 March 1989, B/1–6

36 *Pravda Ukrainy*, 18 February 1989, quoted in *SWB* SU/0400, 4 March
1989, B/7–10

37 Kathleen Mihalisko, 'Police crack down on demonstration in Minsk',
RL 510/88, 16 November 1988; 'Belorussian Popular Front off to a good
start', *RL* 560/88, 12 December 1988; V. Bykov, 'Dubinki protiv
glasnosti?' in *Ogonyok*, no. 47, 19 November 1988, p. 31

38 Bohdan Nahaylo, 'Representatives of non-Russian national movements
establish co-ordinating Committee', *RL*, 22 June 1988; 'Non-Russian
national-democratic movements hold another meeting', *RL* 645/88,
10 October 1988

39 Bohdan Nahaylo, 'Non-Russian democratic movements adopt charter
and issue appeal to Russian intelligentsia', *Report on the USSR*, 1:8,
24 February 1989, pp. 15–17

40 *Current Digest of the Soviet Press*, 40:3, 17 February 1988, p. 4

41 James Critchlow, '"Corruption", nationalism and the native elites in
Soviet Central Asia', *Journal of Communist Studies*, 4:1 (March 1988),
pp. 142–61

42 See Chapter 3; Nancy Lubin, *Labour and Nationality in Soviet Central
Asia* (Princeton University Press, 1984); Alistair McAuley, 'Economic
development and political nationalism in Uzbekistan', *Central Asian
Survey*, 5:3–4 (1986), pp. 161–82; *Pravda*, 14 April 1988; James
Critchlow, 'Desertification of the Aral region: economic and human
damage', *RL* 392/87, 26 August 1987

43 *Literaturnaya gazeta*, 20 January 1988, p. 13

44 Bess Brown, 'Corruption reported flourishing again in Uzbekistan',
RL 492/88, 3 November 1988

45 Ann Sheehy, 'The Alma Ata riots and their aftermath', *RL* 3/87, 23
December 1986; Alistair McAuley, *Civil Disturbances in Alma Ata: a
Comment* (Russian & Soviet Studies Centre, University of Essex,
Discussion Paper no. 8, December 1987)

46 *SWB* SU/0476, 7 June 1989, p. i; *Sunday Times*, 11 June 1989, p. A16;
Independent, 15 June 1989, p. 11

47 Annette Bohr, 'Formation of a People's Front in Tadjikistan', *RL* 498/88,

16 November 1988; *SWB* SU/0343, 24 December 1988, B/5–7; SU/0350, 5 January 1989, B/9–10

48 *SWB* SU/0405, 10 March 1989, B/1–6

49 'Soviet antisemitism unchained: the rise of the "Historical and Patriotic Association Pamyat"', *Institute of Jewish Affairs Research Report*, no. 3 (July 1987), pp. 1–8; Ol'ga Dorenskaya, 'Besy nashego vremeni', *Daugava*, 2/89, pp. 82–91; *Materialy Samizdata*, AS 6079

50 One is reproduced by a recipient, Grigorii Baklanov, chief editor of *Znamya* in his journal, 10/88, p. 233

51 *Materialy samizdata*, AS 6079, p. 1

52 For an analysis which is very sensitive to the dangers presented by such an alliance, see Alexander Yanov, *The Russian Challenge* (Oxford, Basil Blackwell, 1987)

53 On the face of it, this is an implausible claim, in view of the fact that Vikulov in 1969 signed a letter which helped to bring about Tvardovskii's downfall. But in a conversation with me in December 1988, Vladimir Lakshin, Tvardovskii's deputy at that time, substantially confirmed it. Lakshin told me that Tvardovskii was not the man to bear a grudge, and was anxious above all to see good literature flourish

54 This distinction is fully explored in John Dunlop, *The Faces of Contemporary Russian Nationalism* (Princeton University Press, 1983)

55 V. Soloukhin, 'Pochemu ya ne podpisalsya pod tem pis'mom', *Nash sovremennik*, 12/88, pp. 186–9

56 V. Kozhinov, 'Pravda i istina', *Nash sovremennik*, 4/88, pp. 160–75

57 V. Kozhinov, 'Samaya bol'shaya opasnost', *Nash sovremennik*, 1/89, pp. 141–75, especially p. 147

58 M. Antonov, 'Na perelome', *Moskva*, 3/88, pp. 3–26, especially 5–6

6 Religion and the atheist state

1 *Pravda*, 30 April 1988, p. 1

2 A. Krasnov-Levitin, *Ruk tvoikh zhar* (Tel-Aviv, Krug, 1979), p. 102

3 Jane Ellis, *The Russian Orthodox Church: a contemporary history* (London, Croom Helm, 1986), p. 14

4 V. Zelinskii, *Prikhodyashchie v tserkov'* (Paris, La Presse Libre, 1980), p. 46

5 Ellis, pp. 215–17

6 D. Pospielovsky, 'The survival of the Russian Orthodox Church in her millennial century; faith as *martyria* in an atheistic state', paper delivered

at the conference on *Christianity in the Eastern Slav Lands*, School of
Slavonic & East European Studies, University of London, July 1988

7　Moshe Lewin, 'Popular religion in twentieth-century Russia', in his *The Making of the Soviet System* (London, Methuen, 1985), pp. 57–71

8　V. Rasputin, *Farewell to Matyora* (New York, Macmillan, 1979)

9　Jane Ellis, 'USSR: the Christian seminar', *Religion in Communist Lands*, 8 (1980), pp. 92ff

10　Ellis, *Russian Orthodox Church*, Ch. 13

11　Interview with Metropolitan Filaret of Minsk, 5 May 1988

12　Yu. A. Rozenbaum, 'K razrabotke proekta zakona SSSR o svobode sovesti', *Sovetskoe gosudarstvo i pravo*, 2/89, pp. 91–8

13　W. Sawatsky, *Soviet Evangelicals since World War II* (Kitchener, Ontario, Herald Press, 1981), pp. 241–2

14　*Ibid.*, pp. 107, 177–9

15　Rev. Michael Bourdeaux, *Religious Ferment in Russia: Protestant opposition to Soviet religious policy* (London, Macmillan, 1968), pp. 117–19

16　On Baptist numbers, see Christel Lane, *Christian Religion in the Soviet Union: a sociological study* (London, Allen & Unwin, 1978), pp. 140–1

17　For general studies of Islam in the Soviet Union, see especially A. Bennigsen & C. Lemercier-Quelquejay, *Islam in the Soviet Union* (London, Pall Mall, 1967); M. Rywkin, *Moscow's Muslim Challenge: Soviet Central Asia* (London, M. E. Sharpe, 1982)

18　A. Bennigsen & S. Enders Wimbush, *Mystics and Commissars: Sufism in the Soviet Union* (London, C. Hurst & Co, 1985)

19　Taras Kuzio, 'Opposition in the USSR to the occupation of Afghanistan', *Central Asian Review*, 6 (1987), pp. 99–117

20　Vasyl Markus, 'Religion and nationalism in Ukraine', in Pedro Ramet (ed.), *Religion and Nationalism in Soviet and East European Politics*, 2nd edn (Durham, North Carolina, Duke University Press, 1989), pp. 138–70

21　*Observer*, 30 October 1988, p. 29; Ivan Hvat, 'The Ukrainian Catholic Church, the Vatican and the Soviet Union during the pontificate of Pope John Paul II', *Religion in Communist Lands*, 11:3 (winter 1983), pp. 264–80

7 The paradox of Gorbachev's reforms

1 Dev Murarka, *Gorbachev: the limits of power* (London, Hutchinson, 1988), pp. 54–6; V. P. Gagnon, Jr., 'Gorbachev and the collective contract brigade', *Soviet Studies*, 39:1 (January 1987). pp. 1–23; for the frustration of earlier experiments of this kind, see A. Yanov, *The Drama of the Soviet 1960s: a lost reform* (Berkeley, California, Institute of International Studies, 1984)
2 Murarka, p. 241
3 *Ibid.*, p. 239
4 *Materialy samizdata*, AS 5785, pp. 1–3
5 John Dunlop, 'The almost-rehabilitation and re-anathematization of Aleksandr Solzhenitsyn', *Working Papers in International Studies*, Hoover Institution, Stanford University, February 1989
6 Walter Laqueur, 'Glasnost', *Commentary*, 86:1 (July 1988), pp. 13–24
7 *Pravda International*, 12 (1988):7, p. 36
8 Philip Hanson, 'The Economy', in Martin McCauley (ed.), *The Soviet Union under Gorbachev* (London, Macmillan, 1987), pp. 97–117
9 V. Selyunin, 'Revansh byurokratii', in Yu. Afanas'ev, *Inogo ne dano* (Moscow, Progress, 1988), p. 199
10 At a meeting of the Presidium of the Council of Ministers, 29 July 1988, SWB SU/0217, 30 July 1988, C/3
11 Otto Latsis, 'Ugroza perestroike', *Znamya*, 7/88, p. 178
12 *Pravda*, 6 March 1989, p. 3
13 Karl-Eugen Wädekin, 'Agriculture', in Martin McCauley (ed.), *The Soviet Union under Gorbachev*, pp. 118–34
14 See Gorbachev's speech at the 19th Party Conference, SWB SU/0191, 30 June 1988, C/4–5
15 SWB SU/0411, 17 March 1989, C/3–20
16 *Pravda*, 16 January 1989, p. 1
17 See for example A. Kazarina, 'Vina?', *Literaturnaya gazeta*, 11 January 1989, p. 11
18 SWB SU/0351, 6 January 1989, C/1–12
19 Afanas'ev, *Inogo ne dano*, p. 199
20 Marshall Goldman, *USSR in Crisis: the failure of an economic system* (New York, Norton, 1983), pp. 77, 110–11
21 Soviet television, 15 September 1988, SWB SU/0261, 20 September 1988, C/11
22 At the 19th Party Conference: SWB SU/0195, 5 July 1988, C/9
23 *Sovetskaya kul'tura*, 2 April 1987, p. 2

24 Mikhail Gorbachev, *Perestroika: new thinking for our country and the world* (London, Collins, 1987), pp. 146–7

25 Address to the UN General Assembly, New York, 7 December 1988: *SWB* SU/0330, 9 December 1988, C1/1–4

26 *Pravda*, 8 January 1989, p. 2

27 A. Tsipko, 'Istoki stalinizma', *Nauka i zhizn'*, 11/88, p. 55

28 V. Medvedev, 'K poznaniyu sotsializma', *Kommunist*, 17/88, p. 8

29 R. Conquest (ed.), *Justice and the Legal System in the USSR* (London, Bodley Head, 1968), pp. 13–21

30 *Pravda*, 5 July 1988

31 Conversation with Aleksandr Ogorodnikov, 17 December 1987

32 *Izvestiya*, 29 July 1988, p. 2

33 *Pravda*, 11 April 1989, p. 1

34 *Independent*, 3 February 1989; 11 April 1989; 22 April 1989

35 Dawn Mann, 'Elections to the Congress of People's Deputies nearly over', *Report on the USSR*, 14 April 1989

36 E. g. Tolpezhnikov from Riga, *SWB*, SU/0470, 31 May 1989, C/11

37 *SWB*, SU/0468, 29 May 1989, C/1, 3–4

38 *SWB*, SU/0475, 6 June 1989, C/2

39 *Observer*, 4 June 1989, p. 25

40 *SWB*, SU/0470, 31 May 1989, C/2–3

41 *Ibid.*, C/9–10

42 *Independent*, 30 May 1989, p. 12

43 *Independent*, 1 June 1989, p. 10; *Sunday Times*, 4 June 1989, p. B9

44 L. Batkin, 'Vstrecha dvukh mirov na s"ezde deputatov', *Moskovskie novosti*, 11 June 1989, p. 9

45 *New York Times Review of Books*, 35:20, 22 December 1988, pp. 28–9

46 *Izvestiya*, 8 June 1989, p. 6. It is true that Rasputin moderated Stolypin's tone somewhat. Stolypin's last sentence read 'We want a great Russia.'

Index

177

Index

Index

Index

Rasputin, Valentin 52–3, 56, 110, 117, 155–6
rationing 16–17
reform,
  agricultural 126–7, 134–6
  economic 3, 17–18, 45, 93, 104, 109, 132–8, 154–5
  electoral 3, 70–1, 73, 145, 146, 149–50, 152
  legal 144–7
  necessity of 7
  opposition to 1–2, 17
  political 3, 8, 93, 139–40, 145, 146–51
religion,
  and nationalism 84, 88
  post-Stalin 41, 49
  and reform 145
  and social solidarity 112–15, 121–2, 124
  and Tsarism 31–3
'revivalists' 107–10, 155
revolution, Russian 24, 32–6, 77–8, 107–9, 131
river diversions 50, 54–6, 61, 101, 103, 130
Rodionov, General 150, 151
Russian Orthodox Church 31–2, 68, 104, 106, 107, 113–20, 122, 124–5
Russians 52, 72, 80, 93, 104–10, 154–6
Rybakov, Anatolii 108
Ryzhkov, Premier 134

St Petersburg Soviet 25
Sajudis (the Movement) 60, 91, 93, 99, 149, 156
Sakharov, Andrei 3, 43–4, 52, 59, 129, 147–8, 150–1
samizdat 5, 39, 41, 65, 97
Schapiro, Leonard 151
scholars, and nationalism 81, 83–4
Schumacher, Ernst 109
science,
  and dissent 43–5, 52, 55–6, 61
  and nationalism 88
  and revolution 33–4, 35–6
secession, right of 86, 90
security police 8, 30, 110–11, 150, 154
  and protest movements 62
  under Stalin 5, 15–16, 35, 37
self-determination 78
Selyunin, V. 134, 137
semiotics 45

Sergii, Metropolitan 113–14
Shalamov, Varlam 9
Shcherbak, Yurii 97, 98
Shcherbitskii, V. 95, 161
Shevardnadze, Edvard 87
Shmelyov, N. 109
Sholokhov, Mikhail 52
Sinyavskii, Andrei 39–41
skhod 22–3, 26
sobornost (spirit of community) 113, 115, 118, 122
socialism, under Gorbachev 70, 138–9, 141, 144–5
socialist realism 35–6
society, created by party 9–10, see also civil society
Soloukhin, Vladimir 108, 131
Solovyov, Yurii 73
Solzhenitsyn, Alexander 47–8, 100, 131, 157
Songaila, Ringaudas 91
Soviet Committee for the Protection of Peace 61
Soviet Sociological Association 66
Soviet Union, imperial structure 2, 77–8, 107
Soviet of Workers' Deputies 25
soviets 3, 24–7, 29, 111, 152
Stalin, Josef,
  and intelligentsia 34–6, 37–8, 107
  memorial to victims 67, 99
  and nationalism 80–1
  opposition to 1
  and religion 114–15, 124
  system 5, 8–9, 14–15, 129
  terror 46, 99, 107, 108, 130–1
starosta (elder) 23, 24
Stepniak 23
Stolypin, Peter 155
Stus, Vasyl' 97
Sufi brotherhoods 122, 123

Tadjikistan 100
technology, gap 2
Tocqueville, A. de 76
totalitarianism ix, 5–13, 27–8, 30–1, 36, 52, 68, 151–3
  crisis of 1–2, 14, 75
  resistance to 100
trade unions 43
Trust Group 61–3
Tsipko, A. 141
Turchin, Valentin 3

Index

Turkmenia 100
Tvardovskii, Alexander 46–8, 107

Ukraine 60, 80, 93–8, 99, 114
Ukrainian Catholic Church 124–5
Ukrainian Culturological Club 97–8, 156
Union of Evangelical Christians and
  Baptists 120
urbanisation 3–4, 28, 48–9
US, Strategic Defence Initiative 2
Usmankhodzhaev, Inamzhon 102
Uzbekistan 100, 102, 103

Vaino, Karl 89, 91
Vazgen, Catholicos 84
Vendrov, Academician 54
Vikulov, Sergei 107
'village prose' 48–9, 107
Vlasov, Yurii 150
Voinovich, Vladimir 12

weaponry 2
women, in education 4
workers 16, 24–7, 43, 137–8
  rights 70

writers 39–40
  and dissent 43, 45–7, 52–3, 55, 59,
    61
  and nationalism 76, 81, 83–4,
    89–90, 103, 107, 108
  and reform 130
  and religion 120
  rural 48–9, 107
Writers' Unions 11, 35–6, 55–6, 63, 96–9
  of RSFSR 106–7, 138–9

Yakovlev, Alexander 106
Yanshin, Academician 56
Yaroshinskaya, Alla 73
Yel'tsin, B., *see* El'tsin
youth 1, 4
  and reform 63–6, 71
  and religion 117–20

Zalygin, Sergei 56, 107, 156
Zaslavskaya, Tatyana 45, 66, 106, 109
Zel'dovich, Academician 52
Zinoviev, Alexander 11, 29–31

Index compiled by Meg Davies (Society of Indexers)